"Nicki Scully is a true modern day shaman who demonstrates a rare gift for leading us into the realms of magic which inspire and transform. Her ability to artistically weave evocative images enhances the well-documented evidence that guided imagery strengthens healing and personal growth."
—Rev. Sonia Sierra Wolf, Healing Hypnosis and Spiritual Guide, and Fred Alan Wolf, Ph.D., author of *Mind into Matter: A New Alchemy of Science and Spirit*

"For anybody who is interested in broadening their life quite instantly—faster than going to Egypt or Bali—these inner journeys will help you retrain your consciousness and have at your fingertips a whole array of archetypal energies."
—Gay Luce, Ph.D., author of *Body Time* and *Your Second Self*

"Nicki's light and playful approach is a relief from some of the more common versions of creative visualization. . . . I can imagine using it as an oracle that falls open to whatever page it selects, showing a message for the day, reminding us of our essential animal nature."
—Vicki Noble, author of *Motherpeace: A Way to the Goddess*

"Nicki Scully has managed to translate her vast knowledge of Egypt's archetypal gods and goddesses into journeys for the seeking soul, where the ancient path becomes relevant to this most difficult present. The journey of life to self-fulfillment not only becomes a path for self-healing, but also helps empower one to help and to heal others and all living things."
—Oh Shinnah, Native American healer

"In this remarkable book, Nicki Scully takes her readers through various initiations, rituals, and shamanistic journeys. . . . Those who take the journey with her will find it challenging, enriching, and rewarding."
—Stanley Krippner, Ph.D., Professor of Psychology at Saybrook Institute and coauthor of *Personal Mythology* and *Dreamworking*

"The natural history of mythic images presented in Nicki Scully's *Power Animal Meditations* brings myths to life, allowing them to open inner doors, activate energies, impart wisdom, and move the reader to action."
—James A. Swan, Ph.D., author of *Sacred Places* and associate professor of anthropology at the California Institute of Integral Studies

WERNEKE © 2001

POWER ANIMAL MEDITATIONS

SHAMANIC JOURNEYS WITH YOUR SPIRIT ALLIES

NICKI SCULLY

ILLUSTRATED BY ANGELA WERNEKE
FOREWORD BY ROWENA PATTEE KRYDER

Bear & Company
Rochester, Vermont

Bear & Company
One Park Street
Rochester, Vermont 05767
www.InnerTraditions.com

Library of Congress Cataloging-in-Publication Data

Scully, Nicki, 1943-
    Power animal meditations : shamanic journeys with your spirit allies / Nicki
    Scully ; illustrated by Angela Werneke.
        p. cm.
    Rev. ed. of: The golden cauldron. c1991.
    ISBN 1-879181-71-1
        1. Shamanism. 2. Animals—Miscellanea. 3. Thoth (Egyptian deity) 4. Totems.
    5. Symbolism. 6. Spiritual exercises. I. Scully, Nicki, 1943- Golden cauldron. II.
    Title.
BF1621 .S375 2001
299'.93—dc21

                                                                    2001043426

Printed and bound in Canada

10 9 8 7 6 5 4 3 2 1

Text design and layout by Mary Anne Hurhula
This book was typeset in Garamond with Lithos as the display typeface

To the healing of Mother Earth
and to all my relations

SPECIAL NOTICE
TO THE READER

Although this book suggests experiences that can result in healing, it is not meant to give specific recommendations for the treatment of particular illnesses, either physical or emotional. This book explores a variety of alternative possibilities that are meant to be used as adjunctive approaches to conventional modalities and are not intended to replace recognized therapies or medical diagnosis and treatment. It is suggested that the reader approach these journeys with caution, for they, as with any deep explorations of the psyche, can sometimes catalyze states of emotional intensity.

CONTENTS

Part III: Journeys for Awakening

Part IV: Journeys for Transformation

Part V: Healing Journeys

Part VI: Journeys for Exploration

Part VII: Journeys for Celebration & Honoring

Part VIII: Journeys for Liberation

Afterword

Acknowledgments

This kind of work is never done in isolation: it takes a group effort, with each person contributing a crucial piece in order to create the whole. In both the first and second editions, every guided meditation was inspired through the focus of students and friends who made the initial totem animal connections. They then journeyed with me to clarify the specific experiences that each totem wanted to offer these pages.

I would like to give special thanks to the following people, whose focus and attention helped bring this work to life: Roland Barker, Jane Bell, Anita Bermont, Lief Caroon, Bo Clark, Gayle Clayton, Christine Coulter, Normandi Ellis, Steve Harter, Charla Hermann, Myrrah, Gloria Taylor-Brown, Kalita Todd, Kay Cordel Whittaker, Paul Wolf, and all the students and friends who took these journeys and gave me their feedback.

Boundless appreciation goes to Barbara Hand Clow and Gerry Clow for believing in the importance of this work and to my editor, Laura Schlivek, for her clear insights.

Deepest gratitude and devotion goes to my husband, Mark Hallert, without whose constant vigilance, support, and keen vision I never could have accomplished this work. And finally, I offer many blessings of love and gratitude to my teacher and mentor, Thoth, and to all the totems and deities who have shared their wisdom and teachings in this book.

PREFACE TO
THE SECOND EDITION

In its first edition, this book was published as *The Golden Cauldron,* which refers to the internal alchemical process used for connecting to your power animal totems in a safe and effective way. Although the title has changed to emphasize the animal guides, I have retained the use of the Cauldron in the text as a symbol of the alchemical beaker that we access within ourselves when we journey into the spirit world.

I strongly suggest that before you jump into these meditations, you read the introductory material and the chapters in Part I. These will give you a deeper understanding of how the journeys in this book actually work as a *process* for achieving transformation. Once you have learned the alchemy and language, you will find that although the journeys have been arranged in specific groupings, you can take any journey that is of interest, without regard to consecutive order.

Since the publication of the first edition, I (along with a circle of students and friends) have conducted ongoing research into the expansion of consciousness. This research has included numerous encounters with intelligent totemic beings, which have provided healing, spiritual advancement, and accurate and beneficial guidance for my students and myself. As a culmination of our research, seven new journeys have presented themselves for inclusion in this second edition.

Our human biological inheritance includes evolutionary lessons from all of the species with whom we share this blessed Mother Earth. Every chemical that we manufacture in our bodies, even those related to our emotions, was first explored and developed by another living entity eons ago. For example, we know now that plants contain brain chemicals. So an animal's teachings are not simply an apt metaphor—they literally tune us in to the reality of what we have inherited from that creature. As we journey with that animal, the abiding wisdom of its species, based on its evolutionary history, awakens the same wisdom in ourselves.

The deeper teaching—and this applies to all the plants and animals—is that what we choose to call a metaphor is actually the traces of a universal form. When we say the web of the spider is a metaphor for the ego, that is really not different from saying that the spider, in its evolution, laid the groundwork that made it possible for the ego as we know it to be born. It is part of what we inherit from the spider.

It is also important to remember that although the new section, "Journeys for Liberation," completes this book, the entire collection of *Power Animal Meditations* is open-ended, and thus will always be a work in progress. The journeys printed here represent my initial explorations into the wisdom of the animals, as they have chosen to present themselves for this work. Each animal has much to teach us. You may repeat any of the journeys in this book as many times as you like. As you return again and again to deepen your relationships in the totemic world, your power animal guides will continue to reveal wider and more diverse ranges of experience.

May your Cauldron be filled with love and wisdom, and may the intelligence of the totems accessible through these pages grace your life and bring you to a deep and clear understanding of your self and all your relations.

With continued dedication to peace and healing,
Nicki Scully
June 14, 2001

FOREWORD TO
THE FIRST EDITION

*The Golden Cauldron** is not only a tool for healing, but a passageway
into the human primordial, numinous experience that touches our past
and has the power to deliver us to a wholesome future. In this book, you
will find a host of guided journeys that can enable you to plumb the
depths of your psyche and the energies of the universe. It is a book not
only to be read, but to be used. (I have found it helpful to lie on the
floor and have someone read the journeys so that the psyche is free to
explore.) This book can help empower you to be more of who you are.
Through your own participation in *The Golden Cauldron,* you can develop
your relationship between the numinous experience and the animal, plant,
and mineral kingdoms. Such processes are a form of deep ecology.

The Cauldron is the crucible of our own bodies, souls, and minds
when we are deeply in touch with our divine self as well as our natural
self: The journeys and preparations in this book are witnesses of the
spirit in Nature. We in the West have long divided spirit and matter so
that an internal war is waged that longs for healing. This internal war
is a root cause of our external conflicts, which collectively become wars
between nations. Nature is our healer, and the spirit is our guide.
Through the Cauldron process, you can access the muse of inspiration
by being guided into the essence of Nature herself. The gods and
goddesses that are archetypally the substrata of Nature as well as of our

---

*In its first edition, *Power Animal Meditations* was entitled *The Golden Cauldron.*

own being are powers that enable the Cauldron process to nourish, transmute, and heal our souls.

As you take these well-guided journeys, you have the opportunity to make allies of the archetypes that transcend time and space yet influence our daily lives. The Cauldron helps us get in touch with ourselves through alchemical processes that can connect the thread of tribal and ancient lineages, rooted in the nature spirits, with our powers of creativity. Divine creativity is primary insofar as it is a re-creation within creation. When you plunge to the depths of the Cauldron, you can emerge with a wealth of allies to help you re-create your life in harmony with Nature and your divine source.

Rowena Pattee Kryder, Ph.D.
Mount Shasta, California
January 1991

Rowena Pattee Kryder is the author of *Sophia's Body, Tiger and Dragon I Ching,* and *Sacred Ground to Sacred Space.* She is the program director of Creative Harmonics Institute in Mount Shasta, California.

INTRODUCTION

This book is the fulfillment of a promise I made to find and share tools for healing. Commitment slid quietly into my life one day in the early 1970s as I stood on a hilltop doing a prayer ceremony with my good friend and one of my first teachers, Oh Shinnah. I felt the strength and power of the ceremony and was impressed by her prayers. In my attempt to sound as eloquent as Oh Shinnah, I found myself parroting her, making lofty promises and committing myself to a life in service to the healing of Mother Earth.

That moment marked a major change in the direction of my life. Because of the power of that commitment, ritualized to make an especially deep imprint on my subconscious mind, I began attracting tools in order to accomplish that statement of purpose. Early on, I learned that if I didn't use the gifts I was given, they would be lost in one way or another. Little by little, as I continued to say "yes" to the spiritual doorways that opened before me, I found myself on a path of continual return, a return to an awareness long lost in the broken pathways of history.

Uprooted and transplanted, many of us have lost the threads of any cohesive traditional roots. We are finding our ways back to the future of our dreams and the magic of our past. We are mending the wheel of life, weaving the old, the new, and the not-yet-discovered into a tapestry that will reflect our collective dreams and visions.

There is no longer any question as to the urgency of our situation here on planet Earth. Every continent is rife with suffering. War is rampant. There are political wars, religious wars, drug wars, and street wars. Disease is pandemic: sexual diseases, environmental diseases, psychoses, and stress-related emotional imbalances pervade society and undermine the collective immune system. Our resources are being squandered by a populace mesmerized by rhetoric from the avatars of greed who govern nations while being blinded by their petty power struggles. The very air we breathe is becoming a nonrenewable resource as the lumber/paper/cattle companies and short-sighted governments continue to destroy old-growth and rain forests throughout the world. Tens of thousands of species of animal and plant life have been made extinct by human encroachment, while thousands more are currently threatened with extinction. Each species is a functioning participant in the ongoing game of life. Valuable medicines whose uses haven't even been discovered vanish before the onslaught of our misguided civilization.

Yet our mistakes and illnesses are our teachers. They bring us the gift of pressure and motivation for change. Pressure transforms coal into diamonds. Similarly, the management of pressure in our personal lives leads to mastery over ourselves and the conditions we have created. We have choice. As problem-solving entities, we can see our collective diseases for the lessons they bring and make the changes required to avoid our own demise. What we create in our microcosmic reality, our personal lives, is reflected in our families, our communities, and, ultimately, the world.

Once we move beyond the fatalistic attitude of victim, we face the awesome challenge of creating the highest quality of life that is available through our inherent ingenuity. The first stage is recognizing the magnitude of our problems. Tremendous potential energy is lost because the priorities of most people are wrapped up in personal day-to-day survival without cognizance of the relationship between personal survival and planetary continuance.

Once planetary problems are seen as personal challenges, we move to the next stage: commitment. How can one single person be effective in dealing with the formidable implications of our widespread difficulties? We are brought up to believe that we are powerless, that there is always someone else who knows more about every subject. Most of us were never told that answers dwell within or that we have intrinsic sensibilities that, when developed and honored, carry us unerringly toward truth. We were taught to deny our feelings and emotions, ignore our instincts, block our intuition, and view imagination as something to be hidden or turned off. After all, the phrase "It's only your imagination" has been a mainstay of subtle parental oppression for generations.

We do create our future, whether or not we choose to do so in a conscious way. We have the option of sleepwalking through the process, unaware of our influence. Most people simply feel that they are victims of circumstance. Only through looking at the larger perspective does one begin to see the relationships and realize the connections between thoughts and action, dreams and reality, cause and effect. As one's consciousness expands, less obvious relationships become apparent and synchronicity appears. When we pay attention to the synchronous events in our lives, we find ourselves at a whole new level of awareness, one tinged with the promise of magic and mystery. Each major change or movement in our development can be marked by a rite of passage.

It is this metaphysical empyrean of magic and mystery to which I wish to introduce the readers of this book. Starting with the development of commitment and moving through to the willingness of each person to take responsibility for his or her own life, we will explore possibilities of personal empowerment. As we pass through the veils that separate the spirit world from ordinary reality, we influence and change our physical existence through interaction with the spirit world. For serious students of the Cauldron, the journeys in this book are rites of passage.

Part I

PREPARATION & INITIATION

It is important to read these chapters before embarking on your journeys. Herein is provided the background and instructions required for a fulfilling and joyous exploration through the inner landscapes of Power Animal Meditations.

THE CAULDRON

The Cauldron, ancient symbol of the cosmic womb, source of all life and wisdom, has figured prominently in history and mythology. Throughout time and in many diverse cultures, this vessel has stood for the place of continuance: It is the churning, boiling receptacle within which all life is returned, remixed, and regenerated in perpetual cycles. The Cauldron is a metaphor for the alchemical beaker in which transformation and healing occurs. We contain this vessel within ourselves, in our abdominal region, or womb. It is through the symbolism of the Cauldron that we are able to transform our perspective to include an awareness of the spirit realm. The Cauldron allows us to connect with our animal totem allies and see the world through their eyes.

The Cauldron we work with in this book is gold, primarily because of the properties of gold. Gold is the purest of substances, and it cannot be tarnished. It is associated with the sun, as a physical manifestation of that which has been worshiped as the life-giving force of creation. Gold, in this context, is also a symbol of service.

The most prevalent surviving myths about the Cauldron are related to paganism, an ancient Goddess-worshiping religion in which the womb of the Goddess was a central theme and provided the source for abundance and healing. The Crone, custodian of the Cauldron, was in ancient times considered a revered healer, seer, mystic, and wise woman who understood the use of herbs and lived in harmony with nature.

This notion has been sadly debased in modern Western culture, for the Crone was turned into an ugly, malefic hag in the linear, patriarchal church/state of the Middle Ages by those who would usurp her wisdom and power. As a result, the idea of a cauldron now often conjures images of a stooped-over old witch, dressed in black with a wart on her chin, and a black cat, back arched and hackles raised, walking the edge of a fence as the old crone stirs the bubbling cauldron.

This change in image has both weakened her position and hidden the true source and magic of nature. One could consider the search for the Holy Grail as the search for the lost Cauldron, for the grace and abundance that vanished when the circle was broken and its priestesses burned at the stakes during the Inquisition.

Various symbolic expressions of the Cauldron appear in a variety of cultural contexts. In China, it is known as the Ting. In the I Ching or Book of Changes, hexagram 50 is "Ting/The Caldron," which suggests the idea of nourishment, preparing food. (See The I Ching or Book of Changes, translated by C. F. Baynes and R. Wilhelm. Princeton, NJ: Princeton University Press, 1969; p. 641.)

> Nothing transforms things so much as the *ting*. . . . The transformations wrought by Ting are on the one hand the changes produced in food by cooking, and on the other, in a figurative sense, the revolutionary effects resulting from the joint work of a prince and a sage. . . . The Caldron means taking up the new.

According to David W. Patten in *The Secrets of the Alphabet, an Alphabet of Ancient Celtic Wisdom* (an as-yet unpublished manuscript), the Celtic cauldron of Cerridwin, the Mother of all creation, symbolically contained an herb for each day of the year. Whoever drank of its contents would possess all knowledge.

Egyptian, Hindu, and Norse mythologies each contain cauldrons symbolizing the female power of cosmic creation. In Egypt, the god Osiris is said to be associated with a heavenly chalice that never runs dry, and the goddess Nephthys, sister of Isis, wears a vessel upon her head. The Norse god Odin, disguised as a serpent, drank from the Wise Blood in the cauldrons of the Great Mother's womb in order to obtain his power.

Kali, the Hindu goddess, is also associated with the Cauldron. The god, Indra stole her power by drinking the elixir from her cauldron, which is said to have given the power of shape-shifting. He, like Odin, turned into a bird to carry the blood back to the other gods of his pantheon. (See *Women's Encyclopedia of Myths and Secrets* by Barbara Walker. San Francisco: Harper & Row, 1983; p. 150.)

The most sacred of objects to the indigenous tribes of the North American plains is the sacred pipe. While the stem of the pipe represents the masculine, creative, generative power that transmits the prayer, the bowl symbolizes the feminine, receptive vessel that is the Earth. It is within this vessel, or cauldron, that the alchemy of the pipe ceremony occurs, the transmutation of the herbs or tobacco into the smoke that carries the prayers to the four directions. When stem and bowl are connected, all things in the universe are connected and functioning in balance.

Many shamanic cultures, especially those of central Asia and Siberia, define the Cauldron as that vessel within which the dismembered body of the initiate is boiled and then later re-membered. Shamans are those who have mastered death through illness, dreams, or visions and have thus come to an experiential understanding of their own immortality. Historically, it is the function of the shaman to intercede with the spirit world in order to effect changes in the physical world, such as healing or changing the weather, in ways that serve their communities. This book is not meant to create instant shamans, for the road to becoming a true shaman is long and arduous. Rather, it offers a conscious use of shamanistic techniques that are effective for rapid personal growth and development.

The Cauldron as a process provides guidance to assist travelers in the spirit world. Our bodies provide vessels for spirit, dwelling places for the divine ones who speak to us in the silence of our search for understanding the great mystery of life. It is our awareness of these beings—deities, archetypes, and totems—that helps them interact with and influence physical reality.

When I was initiated to the Cauldron as a path to be developed as the expression of my work, I did not yet understand the connection between Egypt, the country that is the focus of my personal studies and travel, and this symbolic Cauldron, which I associated primarily with the Goddess traditions. It was June 1986, and I had been working all day with some students, practicing alchemy and advanced healing techniques.

We were taking a break at dusk and were sitting at my dining room table. I was remarking about the problems I was having establishing teaching as the primary support of my family when Thoth, the Egyptian god of wisdom, appeared in his ibis/man form and asked if I would like further work to do. With my good friend, student, and teacher Brian O'Dea as intercessor, Thoth gave me the Cauldron initiation in the same way it is presented in this book in the Cauldron alchemy and the journey with Vulture and the Crone.

The regenerative waters of the Cauldron stirred up almost immediately, yielding a rich stream of nourishing possibilities, as deities and animal totems appeared to offer substance or spice into the rich stew that was brewing. The first several journeys are given in roughly the same order they came to me.

As the work progressed, I began to recognize when new and different totems wanted to bring into the Cauldron a teaching regarding their special attributes. Often, during a class or session, a totem or deity unrelated to the work at hand would send me a message through a student or leave such a strong impression that he or she would feel compelled to mention its appearance. Sometimes in class, but more often later (in privacy at my computer or over the telephone), we would go to Thoth and request permission to visit the new ally, who would then relate to us the specific journey and appropriate background information to include in the continually developing Cauldron teachings. The being would take us through the experience so that we would comprehend whatever attribute it wanted to contribute. This volume, the first opportunity to print a collection of these journeys, represents only a portion of the material available.

I hope you will drink deeply from the Cauldron and in so doing comprehend its infinite source and nature, for the more you drink from its endless fountain of wisdom, the more there will be to nourish you. Once you have developed rapport with Thoth and other allies, you will find it easier to explore on your own, for to explore the Cauldron is to look within the deep mirror of your own consciousness.

DEITIES, TOTEMS, & ARCHETYPES

We are in the process of transforming our identities from linear realities to holographic paradigms in which each fragment contains the whole. Through our observations of nature, we learn about ourselves and our relationship to the wondrous creation of which we are a part. As without, so within: The rich landscapes of nature are reflected in the deep well of introspection, our internal Cauldrons.

To fully understand ourselves is to comprehend our relationship to the abundant forms of life expressed in nature. Humans tend to be both chauvinistic and anthropomorphic. We are sure that we are the most intelligent species, and any concept of supreme being would have to look like us. This limiting notion keeps us from recognizing the vast potential for help and knowledge available to us from our relatives in the plant, animal, mineral, and spirit kingdoms.

In Egypt, the country that inspired many of the journeys in this book, the pantheon is primarily zoomorphic. Most deities relate to animal totems. Animal heads rest on human bodies, human heads on animal bodies, and there are occasional composite creations that are mixtures of related totems. Sometimes the totems are seen through symbols worn on the heads of the gods that describe or symbolize certain functions. The crocodile journey came from Sobek, the crocodile god of Egypt, and the hippopotamus came from Tarät (Taueret), an Egyptian goddess. The cobra also originates in Egypt.

However, *Power Animal Meditations* is nonexclusive. Kuan Yin, from the Orient, and Ganesha, a Hindu god, also have contributed journeys. There are no fences or walls in the Cauldron, no barriers between traditions or geographic locations. All cultures and historical images are accessible through its alchemy.

Universal symbols that crop up in dreams and visions have similar meanings, even in diverse cultures. *Deities* dwell in each person's consciousness as the personification of archetypal aspects of nature. *Archetypes* are expressions of basic and fundamental ideas, such as love or compassion. Deities are the personal and cultural representations of the archetypes. The images of deities are legacies from our ancestors, passed down to us in the various pantheons and cataloged in the rich history of mythology and legend.

In our technological age, we can look back across time and trace the evolution of archetypes from ancient anonymity, through diverse cultural changes and traditions, and into a present rich with the multiplicity of cultural variety. These archetypes, like the Great Mother, express the larger concepts that when personified become the deities like Kuan Yin, Kali, or Isis. The Greek goddess Hecate, for example, is a cultural interpretation of an archetypal crone. The appearances of archetypes vary somewhat between cultures, and one's personal affinities will attract the traditional representation that is suitable in the journeys offered in this book. Although I might suggest an Egyptian entity or a being clothed in Egyptian style, you might be more comfortable with a corresponding guide that will be stronger and clearer for you.

Deities also function as repositories for the loftiest and most potent qualities we wish to honor. We pour our feelings for these attributes into the symbol of the god or goddess in the form of worship or devotion, and we can call that back to us as our personal needs arise. For example, Kuan Yin has been worshiped as a goddess of mercy and compassion for thousands of years in the Orient. Her very name has come to exemplify those qualities. When we call on her, pray to her, or journey with her, Kuan Yin expresses back to us that which she has become through the continuous nourishment of devotion. We give life to the deities through our recognition of their presence in our psyches.

Totems, on the other hand, are more worldly expressions of the qualities or aspects represented by the deities. Everywhere we look in nature we find our own attributes—and those we wish to emulate—mirrored back to us in other life-forms. In prehistoric times, clans were often associated with animal totems that were both revered and modeled by the people of the clan.

Every person has a power animal, and you can develop relationships with many animal totems. Often there is a subconscious link between you and your power animal that expresses itself in your love for its species, even though you are not always aware of its influence in your life. When you have a conscious relationship with a totem, it becomes your ally. Totems are often powerful messengers, healers, and protectors, and they bring great benefit to those who develop and maintain such relationships.

Communication with deities, totems, or archetypes is achieved through resonance, based on congruence between ourselves and beings in other dimensions. The song of our own vibrations, the chord that we generate through our being, harmonizes with and then joins for a moment the field of the being to which we are connecting. Within this resonance the exchange of information takes place. The moment itself exists within a timeless, infinite realm outside our "normal," ordinary reality structure.

The resulting communication is usually experienced through our various sensory mechanisms and can include "mind's eye" and imagination. Occasionally you will have opportunities to experience merging with a totem. When you step into the consciousness of that being, it is like putting on its mask or identity. Often, it is as though you have clothed yourself in the body of your ally, or merged with it, so that you can see through its eyes, which gives you the advantage of the unique worldview and perspective of that being. For example, when journeying with Eagle, you fly quite high, so that you have a more lofty view of the situation you are observing. You also have the benefit of the keen vision that enables an eagle to see quite clearly from a great distance.

Each totem provides specific qualities and attributes that are shared in *Power Animal Meditations*. As you continue to work with those totems with whom you have affinity, you will learn more about them and their unique gifts. The Cauldron alchemy is designed to prepare you so that when you come into this type of union the result will be mutual support and sharing.

In these journeys, connection is often made through eye contact. I've found that expressing communications from your heart center also helps to make the connection stronger. Through the bonding that is established, the totems become our allies—we can work together in a friendly manner.

Allies express themselves through "morphogenetic fields" belonging to their species. This field, named by biologist Rupert Sheldrake, surrounds each member of the species and binds it to its High Self, the larger species "over-self" or totem energy of the species. For example, there is the archetypal Eagle, and there are individual eagles. Each draws from and feeds into the morphogenetic field that contains the collective history of the species of eagles. Current evidence in quantum physics supports the discovery that generation by generation, each species learns through its experience, and that knowledge is stored for use by future generations in its morphogenetic field.

With deities, totems, and archetypes as your guardians and guides, *Power Animal Meditations* provides a method by which you can reach down through your subconscious mind into the collective consciousness, where all aspects of the creation interrelate, and pull up to the surface whatever you need or desire for your next increment of growth. If your intention is clear and pure, the result will be that message, lesson, or experience that is perfect for the moment. The best preparation is to fill your heart with gratitude for the many blessings of life, for a heart filled with gratitude shines a bright light upon the path.

How to Use This Book

This book is meant to be experienced. It is a tool that can be used by all people and allows them to be in their own power. This represents a change from centuries of giving power to beings and idols outside of self. Many of the journeys are actual initiations, rites of passage that can alter one's perception of reality.

For optimum results, create a special space in which to do the work. Preparing that space is like cleaning your house for company, making sure it is comfortable and free of anxieties and distractions. Smudging with sage or cedar, if available (or with incense, if you prefer), helps to clear the environment of inappropriate energies. This involves placing cedar or sage leaves in an abalone shell or other nonflammable receptacle and burning them to create a purifying smoke. It is important to have a door or window partially open while smudging to provide an outlet for unwanted energies. Many Native American tribes smudge themselves, each other, and their sacred spaces and implements.

Extra details like flowers or candles lend a sense of sacredness when intentionally placed. You don't need to complicate this process, for in this practice the most important landscape is *within*. The set and setting must, however, be peaceful and allow you to be comfortable enough to relinquish the cares and concerns of your external reality in favor of the rich possibilities of the internal spirit world.

Alchemy is a transmutational process, used ostensibly by the ancients to turn base metals into gold and to create the elixir of life. In the *Power Animal Meditations* journeys, each of us is the vessel, the alchemical beaker within which the elements of life are mixed and transmutation occurs, changing our state of consciousness so that we can perceive in the spirit realms. The Cauldron alchemy is an active form of meditation. There are no prerequisites beyond clear intention and the ability to pay attention. Attention is the coin of the realms, and you get what you pay for! It is best to avoid distractions and to train yourself to perceive outside noises or unavoidable disruptions as part of the script of your journey.

Each person has his or her unique way of accessing information. Some people are visual, while others are auditory, kinesthetic, or empathic. Some simply "know." I have met healers who can diagnose through their sense of smell. Modern technological culture emphasizes visual and auditory input, and as a result, some of our psychic abilities have atrophied. All of the inner sensibilities can be developed, however, though our preconceptions and preconditionings often get in the way.

Television provides a constant barrage of stimulation, which feeds the notion that sight and sound are our main avenues of reception. And for the most part it does seem that way, although it might be as a result of current lifestyles that allow some of our psychic sensibilities to deteriorate.

Most of the people who study with me are naturally visual. Many are auditory or at least are aware of that ability. Many find that the words used to direct the journeys catalyze feelings or bring up emotions. Equally effective but much more difficult to validate is the "knowing." Knowers are usually looking for *how* they know and often find that difficult to articulate, yet this is the most direct way, for there is no separation between the knower and the known. I know—I'm a knower, too.

What is really important here is to be okay with whichever way you experience these journeys. Let your primary accessing mode flourish, and at the same time open your awareness to your other inner senses.

It is also important to note that for some of you, another being may appear in the place of Thoth. It is important that you be comfortable with whoever fills that role, so don't force the issue. In addition, once you get into a journey, you might notice that it has a life of its own and follows a script different from the one I have written. Generally, it's best to follow what you are given at such times and let my words simply catalyze for you the experience that wants to come to you in the moment.

By the same token, sometimes you will find that the Cauldron you envision is not gold. It may be made of clay, iron, silver, copper, or another substance. It is important to take note of the material of which your Cauldron is made, for it may change, and you can, through your intention, transform it.

You will notice that some of the animals are masculine and others are feminine. I have chosen to use the gender of the particular entity that came to me with the journey. Yours might be different. In most instances, it doesn't matter.

Many people have asked the question "Am I making this up?" Often it appears that way. Imagination is the lightning rod of the magician. It works together with your will and precedes all forms of creation. We all have the faculty of discrimination, which can be developed to distinguish between what we perceive as our own, our "I-Magi-Nation," and what we know as "other."

These journeys work best when perceptions from other dimensions, the spirit realms, take over, yet you must remember that it is all a part of you. You can objectify a symbolic image of some aspect of yourself and place it outside of yourself so that you can have a meaningful interaction. It comes in an identifiable costume, usually one that is culturally comfortable. This objectification is more or less conscious and makes it much easier to relate to the event or message that occurs.

The attributes mentioned in the introductions to each ally represent the wishes of each totem for this work. Other source materials may suggest other qualities and characteristics that are equally valid, for these are complex beings with much to offer. You can explore many of these additional possibilities in subsequent journeys.

It is important to follow the Cauldron alchemy each time you take a journey, at least until Thoth or your guardian spirit guide is instantly accessible. Even once your guides are there for you, it is important to follow certain of the steps, especially grounding and centering, the feeding of your inner heart flame, and the stirring of your Cauldron. You need to receive the purple-black egg and the crown only *once*, though repetition is not harmful. At the end of each journey it is imperative to ground in a physical way. Find a sensation to let you know you are back in your body, such as feeling your feet on the earth or noticing your chest expanding and contracting with your breath.

The purpose of the alchemy is to help you transpose your focus to the rich domain of the collective consciousness, which is the realm of the deities and totem animal powers. Many people perceive this as an out-of-body experience, while others simply observe a shift in consciousness, much like changing the channel on an FM tuner. Either way works and will get you where you need to be.

As you become more confident and want to explore further, ask Thoth to introduce you to other deities and totems that may be of special interest to you. These pages hold but a taste of the nourishment of the Cauldron.

The journeys are designed so that they can take you while you read them to yourself. If you have trouble tuning in deeply while you are doing the reading, try asking a friend to read it to you aloud. Have him or her go over it first so as to be familiar with the timing. Another possibility is to tape record the journey and play it back to yourself. Several of the journeys in this book have been published on audio-cassette tapes, which are described and listed at the back of this book.

Most pauses in the journey are marked by ellipses (. . .). I have added other instructions in italics where needed. "*Pause*" designates a longer pause than usual, one that encompasses more activity or interaction. I recommend that you allow enough time to complete each section of the journey, so you might want to read the entire journey once or twice to get the feel and timing down before you take it for yourself, and especially if you are reading it for others.

It is always best to read the introductions *before* you actually take a journey, to insure a more effective experience. A few of the journeys are quite complex, and some may be scary for beginners. The kinds of changes and transformations available through this work are not always easy. Those journeys that require extra preparation or resolve will have notations in the introductions.

You will notice that at the end of most journeys there is an opportunity to give a gift or offering to the being with whom you have been working. An exchange is not expected, yet people usually feel better if they can give something back in their friendships. Trust your intuition—you will know what to give. Often there is a message in the gift that is given, which could be an additional key to unlocking that particular experience or information from the journey.

The *Power Animal Meditations* journeys are ideal for group work, healing circles, or other times when people get together. Take turns leading your group through the pathways of the Cauldron. Sharing of experiences is very important. It is through sharing that synchronicities are discovered. Often a person will share a unique visionary event only to discover that three others in the circle had almost identical experiences. Hearing other experiences also helps one's personal interpretation.

I recommend that you begin with the first journey in order to connect with Thoth and express your intention, and then proceed in accordance with your needs. You can start at the beginning and work your way through the collection in the order given or, if you have especially compelling issues in your life, try the journeys that most speak to those issues. You might have an affinity for a specific animal; it may even have entered your dreams. That is a totem you might be most comfortable trying, for it has already called to you. Sometimes you might want to just open the book and see what appears.

Power Animal Meditations can also function as an oracle. Focus your intention to succinctly encompass your question. In order to use this tool, you need only be still, allow yourself to trust, and look for the point of truth in your desires and requests. You can then compose your question and look to see which totem might best be able to address the subject of your focus.

Each time you return to a journey, the results will be unique. It is helpful to keep a journal of your experiences, for often you will be given a gift, a glimpse of knowledge, or a symbol that will be more clearly understood several journeys down the road when it is explained or seen in a different context.

The purpose of *Power Animal Meditations* is to heal. There really is no other purpose. It was given to serve all people at a moment in time when we need to help ourselves and one another. The motivation for using the Cauldron alchemy is to bring us back in touch with our love, our relationship to all forms of life, and to the planet on which we live. That's the key to using this book.

WERNEKE © 1991

THOTH

The overriding principle in *Power Animal Meditations,* for the sake of safety and order, is Thoth (Tahuti), the Egyptian god of wisdom, language, communications, healing, science, and more. He is the architect of everything that happens here, the foundation of this work.

In Egypt, Thoth also functions as the scribe of the gods, the one who keeps the records. He was known to the Greeks as Hermes and to the Romans as Mercury, messenger of the gods. His symbol is the caduceus—two serpents entwined around the staff of life, crowned by double wings—expressive of balance in both spirit and earthly realms. For the Egyptians, Thoth represents the highest concept of mind. As such, one must get beyond Thoth to function in the intuitive recesses of the psyche accessed through the Cauldron. Not only does he guard these realms, but he is the gateway itself, guiding you into your experiences and back out of them, the interface between the adventures of *Power Animal Meditations* and your ordinary life.

All who aspire to know the underlying principles of creation, the true seekers of wisdom and knowledge, must ultimately consult the concept of Thoth in some form. He is the great world teacher who guides the spiritual traveler to the source of desired knowledge and information. He also looks after your body when you journey using the Cauldron alchemy and provides a reference point and wise counsel if you have problems or questions during your journeys.

I first encountered Thoth consciously as part of a transmission process, during a journey similar to the ones in this book. I was brought before a council of the Egyptian pantheon in order to be chosen by one who would henceforth be my mentor and teacher. Thoth came forth, though it was some time before I fully understood the many blessings that working directly with him would bring. It is my great honor and privilege to be able to pass that introduction on to those who encounter this book.

Thoth is most often pictured with an ibis head on a man's body, although he can also appear as either man or ibis. The ibis is a marsh bird related to the crane. In ancient times, this bird was prolific along the river Nile, feeding on fish that dwelt among the papyrus, the tall graceful reeds from which paper was made. The fish is an ancient symbol for wisdom, and fish are found in "schools." Much can be learned by watching the ibis as it hunts. It stands for long periods on one leg and sometimes lifts a wing to create a shadow so that it can see deeper into the water.

The dog-headed baboon is another image for Thoth. In this form, he is pictured sitting on the balance of the scales that weigh the heart of the deceased in Egyptian funerary rites. In addition, a very potent, though less common, expression of Thoth is Cobra, which holds great wisdom of Earth and the realms of the subconscious and through which Thoth has shown me many rites of passage.

I might add that Thoth, being a bird and therefore associated with the element air, is a being of great humor. Don't be surprised if he makes light of the work to set you at ease and in order to make it fun. Things don't always have to be serious to be productive, and Thoth is a master of devising interesting yet meaningful experiences whereby you can find the knowledge and information that you seek. He is also the ultimate shape-shifter, a master of disguises. As you become familiar with his distinctive vibration, you will recognize when and how he is playing with you.

If Thoth as a being or concept is uncomfortable for you, his function can be filled by an image that is more harmonious with your individual desires or needs. Usually this will come about automatically. If another being or entity appears in the place of Thoth when you do the alchemy, that being will serve as your spirit guide and hold the place of guardian for the work of the Cauldron. Sometimes this happens spontaneously when there is a particular guide that wants to serve you in that way.

Please note that, to avoid confusion, I will always refer to the being that fills this role as Thoth.

Occasionally other members of the Egyptian pantheon, such as Horus, the hawk-headed god (see Hawk journey), or Anubis, the jackal god (see Jackal journey), may appear. Those who experience Anubis have particular power and impact with the transformative nature of this work. This is not to be taken lightly, for it indicates a connection to deep levels of healing and possibly more of the shadow aspects. Horus is also a strong guide and teacher, bold and bright, like the sun that illumines the day, although he is usually less playful than Thoth. If a different yet recognizable guide presents himself or herself, take some time to find out what you can about that person or animal.

Thoth would like to be recognized for his ibis, human, or other related forms throughout this book. For those who have a hard time with masculine images, know that this is a being who serves the Goddess. He is the Lord of the Moon and, in a sense, the original hermaphrodite. As such, he is perfectly balanced and capable of maintaining androgyny.

Each time you take a journey, it is important to recount your experience with Thoth in order to gain a deeper understanding and interpretation; it is also helpful to write it down. I highly recommend that you keep a journal of your experiences with the material in this book. You will discover that some messages or information will be better understood through subsequent journeys.

The alchemy is the first part of each journey, which takes you into the presence of Thoth. After you have done this first journey, you may choose to follow the shorter form as given in the "Abbreviated Alchemy" chapter. If you prefer, it is fine to repeat the full alchemy as often as you like.

For your first journey, go to Thoth to begin to develop trust in knowing that he will be there during all your journeys. As your relationship with Thoth and your confidence in the journeys grow, you will understand more about the alchemy and how it works. Thoth is the hermetic seal of the Cauldron, which keeps the contents within so that nothing escapes or is lost. He is also the translator. If there is ever a question about what's happening in a journey, he is there to respond to you. As you develop your unique relationship with Thoth, so will you develop your personal method of using *Power Animal Meditations.*

Over time your commitment to these teachings is likely to change. Journey as often as you like to Thoth to reiterate your commitment or to ask questions as needed.

ALCHEMY & INITIATION

[The alchemy takes you into the presence if Thoth. Once you have greeted him, the journey begins. . . .]

Close your eyes, relax, and breathe deeply. Inhale through the small of your back, filling your belly, and exhale through your tailbone into the earth, deepening your connection to Earth, grounding and centering yourself in preparation for your travels into realms beyond space, beyond time. . . . Feel the cycles of your breath. Feel as your body opens to new levels of sensitivity. . . .

Place your hands before you with the palms facing up to receive the gift that is coming to you. It is a purple-black egg, flecked in gold, and it descends from above to rest gently in the palms of your hands. Notice its size, its weight, its substance. This is an etheric egg, an egg of creation. When you are sure of its presence, draw the egg into your abdomen, as though your abdomen is a womb waiting to receive and nurture the egg that you have been given.

Focus your attention on your heart center. Look deep within your heart to find the eternal flame of life that burns within. As you focus on your inner heart flame, begin directing love to make it grow and *feel* as the radiant warmth and light from own heart flame spreads to illuminate your entire being. . . .

Bring your attention to the top of your head. A crown is placed gently there, around your crown chakra, around the top of your head. Notice what it looks like and how it feels. Notice what it is made of. This crown marks the empowerment you are receiving at this time and provides the portal through which your consciousness travels out of and back into your body.

Look once more to see and feel the egg that has been gestating within the womb of your being. Its outer shell is absorbed into your abdominal walls, revealing the Golden Cauldron within. This Cauldron is the source of all life, all wisdom. Feel as it expands to fill your abdomen. . . .

Begin to stir the waters of life in your Cauldron. As you stir these waters, there is a sound that is generated, like the tone of a Tibetan singing bell or a crystal goblet—the frequency and vibration of gold, which resonates throughout your being. Tune to that sound. . . .

As you continue to stir the contents of the Cauldron, the waters begin to rise. The waters are uplifted until they come into contact with the flame in your heart. There will be hissing, bubbling, and crackling as water hits fire and converts to steam. . . . The steam rises. It opens the passageway in your throat, which is the doorway into the shamanic realms, and begins to fill your head. Let your consciousness rise with the steam. Let it merge with the steam in your head. Focus all of your attention, all of your consciousness, within this steam, and, as the pressure builds, the steam will lift your consciousness right up out of your body through your crown. . . .

When you have passed through your crown, look to your left and you will see Thoth, the being who is your guide and guardian for the journeys of the Cauldron. Greet this being with respect. . . .

As you look into his eyes, let yourself experience a sense of connection with Thoth, in whatever form it naturally takes. . . .

Thoth queries, "Why are you here?"

You may feel your heart and mind opening, as questions and thoughts that you have had for a long time begin rising to the surface. You may be surprised at the depth of emotion you feel as your questions and answers formulate. Pay attention to the responses you receive from Thoth. . . . [*Long pause.*]

Thoth will ask you if this is the path you are choosing to take at this time in your life. . . . [*Pause.*] He will take you on a journey now to give you a glimpse of the possibilities of the Cauldron and the assistance that is available within. . . . [*Long pause.*]

When you return from this part of the journey, you can begin to recognize that in choosing to work in this manner, you are choosing to empower yourself.

If you have questions, ask them. . . . [*Pause.*]

Take whatever time you need to complete your interaction with Thoth for now. . . . Be sure to express your gratitude. A simple "thank you" is sufficient. . . .

Thoth will assist you back into your ordinary consciousness through the doorway that is your crown. . . .

Be sure to ground and center, using the grounding breath. Inhale through the small of your back and exhale through your tailbone into the earth. Make sure that you are centered in your physical form before opening your eyes. . . .

ABBREVIATED ALCHEMY

The Cauldron alchemy is the process by which you change your state of consciousness in order to perceive in the spirit realms. It is recommended that you start with the first initiation, which takes you to Thoth, and then continue with the journey to the Crone.

With the exception of the first time you experience the Cauldron alchemy, you can practice the following abbreviated version:

Ground and center, using the breath to fill your belly on the inhale, and then exhale downward, through your tailbone to connect yourself with the earth. . . .

Devote attention to your heart flame, directing love to make it grow and spread its radiance throughout your being, filling you with warmth and light. . . .

Stir the waters within your Golden Cauldron, tuning to the vibratory sound. Notice as the waters rise to meet the flame in your heart, and experience the conversion as the water meets the fire and turns to steam. . . .

The steam rises, opening the shamanic passageway at your throat and filling your head. Place your entire attention within the steam. As it gathers in your head, it will lift your consciousness up through your crown and into your light body. . . .

Thoth is always at your left. . . .

[*Proceed with the journey.*]

As you continue to practice this process, it will become faster and easier to connect to Thoth, until he is but a breath away. It is important, even when access becomes constant, to remember to ground, center, and nourish your heart flame, and to return to a solid connection in this plane, this physical reality, upon completion of each journey.

PART II

FOUNDATION JOURNEYS

These foundation journeys are the basis for Power Animal Meditations. *They help establish your relationship to this work, laying the foundation and establishing journeying habits that will allow you to go further in some of the other sections. It is here that your relationship with your primary guide begins to develop.*

WERNEKE © 1991

VULTURE & CRONE
Intuitive Wisdom

The first teachings of the Golden Cauldron are given by Vulture and the Crone, who represent the wise, primordial part of ourselves that is female. Through the Cauldron, we reach deep within our own psyches and interact directly with this ancient feminine archetype. She is a part of each of us, regardless of gender, and she can help open the way to a deeper understanding of ourselves and the ways of nature.

Vulture is highly respected in Egypt. One of her aspects, the goddess Mut (pronounced "Moot"), is considered self-procreated and is one of the oldest goddess images. All vultures were thought of as female, and you will see images of vultures on the heads of many goddesses as well as on the crown of the Pharaoh, where the vulture represents upper Egypt. Vulture knows when you are truly ready for change, for she watches and waits patiently, and when the time is ripe, she sees the death of the old and devours it so that it can be born again anew.

In the following journey it is Mut, the vulture goddess, who carries you to her temple, the womb of the earth, where you will meet with her priestess, the Crone. It is this Crone, the wise, old female aspect of yourself, who opens your third eye and begins instructing you on the ways of intuition, herbs, and healing.

The Crone is keeper of the storehouse of herbs, and you can always come to her to learn more about herbs and their uses. She will introduce you to new plant allies or remind you of old plant friends that may be needed in your life at this time. If you are unfamiliar with the herbs she shows you, consult an herbal reference book for further information.

Visit the Crone often to gain a deeper understanding of your feminine nature. It is especially auspicious to take this journey during the full moon.

Vulture & Crone Journey

[*Do the Cauldron alchemy. . . .*]

Thoth directs his staff, and when you look to where he is pointing, there is a resplendent vulture. This is the ancient goddess Mut, mother of all, noble in her character and stature. She is the primordial Mother of the pantheon of Egypt. Mut lifts you gently into flight and carries you across the wondrous vistas of our Mother Earth. Notice the landscape that is beneath you as you soar on the currents of the wind. . . .

Mut is taking you to her secret temple. The entrance is hidden, covered in lush green foliage, marked by clear water near its narrow opening. She flies down with you and enters into the earth through the dark passageway. She descends deep into the earth, until she gently sets you down at the bottom of a large cavern, the womb of Mother Earth. . . .

As Mut points toward the ceiling, the cavern lights up with a soft, warm glow so that you can see around you. Notice the details of this place, this womb. What does it look like and feel like? What colors and textures are here? Open all your senses. Listen to the sounds. . . .

You will notice the sound of running water coming from a niche, where it flows sweetly and gently from the walls of the cave. You must cleanse and purify yourself in these sacred waters in preparation for the next stage of your journey. . . .

When you have completed your cleansing ritual, purifying yourself in the flowing waters of the womb, there is a clean robe or garment for you to put on. . . .

Return to the main part of the cavern. There you will meet the Crone, the embodiment of divine wisdom. This wise old woman has been a priestess of Mut for thousands of years, and yet there is a familiarity about her. She is very pleased that you have made this journey. . . .

The Crone begins placing a circle of crystals in the center of the cavern. As she places each crystal, the cavern comes alight until there is a sacred circle of glowing crystal lights. She beckons you into the center of the circle. The ground churns beneath your feet, yet you find you can maintain your balance.

As you stand before the Crone, she reaches into a fold in her garment and brings forth a magical stone. This stone is the universal medicine, the Healing Stone that contains all knowledge of Earth and her history. How to understand its nature will be revealed through your experience. The Crone shows you the stone and then places it in your third eye, in the center of your forehead. Feel the stone enter and begin to awaken ancient memories and long-forgotten knowledge. . . . [*Pause.*]

The Crone now presents you with an herb, a plant that is a power plant for you. It may be the entire plant or a portion of it—a blossom, a leaf, a root. . . . As you receive this plant, its essence fills you with awareness of its nature. It permeates your being, and you feel it in all the cells of your body. You feel and understand its power. You smell its fragrance, and your mouth is filled with the taste of your new ally. You will know how and when to use this herb for healing yourself or others. . . .

In gratitude for the gifts the Crone has given you, you may wish to give her an offering. You can choose an aspect of yourself, of your physical being or your character, as a gift to support her in her work. . . .

The Crone has a special instruction or initiation that is just for you, according to your own readiness and personal commitment at this time. Receive what she gives to you. . . . [*Long pause.*]

When this time with the Crone is complete, you have only to look deep within her eyes to reconnect with the vibrations of the vulture goddess Mut, and you can carry yourself up and out of this sacred temple. As you fly back over the rich variety of Earth's landscapes, look down and notice any changes in your perception. . . .

Return to the gateway where Thoth awaits. He has been guarding your body while you have traveled in this way. Take a moment to communicate with him about your experience or to ask any questions that may have come up during your journey. . . . [*Pause.*]

Thoth will show you the way back into your body through your crown. . . . Feel yourself connect with your physical body. Take a moment to ground and center yourself, feeling that you are solidly within your body. . . . When you're ready, open your eyes.

WERNEKE © 1991

TREE
Grounding

The tree of life is an ancient and universal symbol, representing and incorporating the fullness of life's cycles. It provides a perfect model for the three primary aspects of ourselves, which in the Huna tradition of the Polynesians are the High, the Middle, and the Low, or Hidden, Selves. The High Self is one's overself or parent self, and it is connected to all the other High Selves. Metaphorically, it can be expressed in the canopy of the tree, reaching for the heights of spirit beyond the bounds of physical limitations. The trunk is like the Middle Self, rational and thinking. It stands for the unique part of ourselves that thinks it is separate. Even as the canopies blend, the trunks are seen as individuated. The root system, hidden beneath the soil of the earth, provides our support and sustenance and corresponds to the Low Self, or subconscious mind, where our history and memories are stored and from where our intuitive powers arise.

Have you ever walked through a forest, or even a local park or your backyard, and talked to trees? The wisdom of trees defies explanation. When you are sad, hug a tree, and it will somehow share your sadness with you and then leave you feeling better.

There is a technique that I often teach in my healing classes in which, after greeting and establishing a relationship with a tree, you can ask your tree friend to help you with healing or with emotional clearing. It is important to ask first, although I have never as yet had a tree turn me down. Then, place both hands on the surface of its trunk and allow the tree to take away your pain, your anger, or your sorrow. You will feel it begin to draw the undesirable energy from you, as though tugging, until the appropriate release is achieved. It is very important when using this technique to open yourself to receive light to fill and replace any energy that is given to the tree. You have only to ask that a ray of light be generated into your being as the release is occurring. Be sure to leave an offering for the tree, even if all you have is the waters of your body.

Trees provide a great opportunity for grounding. At any time as you go about your life, when the winds of change or chaos blow around you, drop into the image of your tree and follow your roots deep into the earth so that you feel stable and secure within yourself. Your roots will go as deep as you will let them.

The following journey can be done over and over again, with many options for experimentation and change, so that along with grounding you can receive healing and information about yourself. Pay attention to the health of your tree, the vibrancy of its color, and the way it holds itself in the world. Notice the season, the time of day or night, and any other significant indications. You will see how aspects of yourself glow in time as you continue to work with the image of your tree body.

Tree meditations lend themselves well to group energies. Natural circles of trees may have been the first temples, even before stone circles were built. Try making a human circle as a grove of trees, and notice how your roots entwine about the roots of the other trees in the grove to give mutual support to one another. Individuals can enter the center of the sacred circle of trees that you create and pray or receive guidance or healing. If you are part of an ongoing circle, you can develop a power circle that can be contacted by any member at any time for healing, rejuvenation, or simply support to get through a difficult time.

Tree Journey

[*First do the Cauldron alchemy. . . .*]
Thoth takes you to a grove in a forest or a place where there is a particular tree with which you have affinity. As you look at this tree, notice how you can read its history in the way it stands. Notice the season and which part of the yearly cycle of growth the tree is in. What kind of tree is this? Is it evergreen or deciduous? Notice whether your tree is solitary, a part of a grove or orchard, or in a deep forest or jungle.

Let the details of your surroundings come into focus so that you can hear and feel as well as see images of the setting. . . .

As you stand before this tree, take a moment to greet it and to share breath. The Hawaiian word *aloha* means "hello," "love," and "to share breath." In this action there is also an honoring of our symbiotic relationship with trees, especially with regard to the oxygen cycle. . . .

Reach out to touch its bark and its leaves or needles. Feel its texture. Now move in closer and embrace your tree, feeling yourself merging with and becoming the tree. . . .

Your consciousness expands to fill the space of the tree's perimeters. The entire vibrational quality has changed as you begin to view the world from the perspective of this tree. Notice how you reach out into the world through your branches and how your roots dig deep into the earth to support you.

Let your consciousness enter and follow the course of your root system, first noticing how the more shallow roots spread to strengthen your foundation. Find and follow a deep tap root as it extends down into the earth, moving around or through the different obstacles that might come up along the way. Notice the different layers of strata, the rocks and minerals you pass, and the variety of textures under the ground. You might even see some crystals, flashing and lighting the way as the terrain becomes denser, darker. . . .

The earth becomes moist as you approach a source of water. Reach out with the tiny filaments at the tip of your root and draw the life-giving water into your root system. Feel yourself swell with the waters of life as you draw this moisture upward. It rises within your roots, back up through the course you have followed, all the way to where your trunk bursts forth from the ground. Let your consciousness rise with the moisture, up the inside of your trunk to your heights and out through all your branches and limbs to the very tips, including your leaves or needles. . . .

From this new vantage point, feel the vibrancy of your tree. A breeze ventures through the grove and circulates around you. Dance with the wind. Listen to its song. Become aware of how trees communicate with their environment. . . . Allow yourself to experience the process of photosynthesis as the sun shines upon your green parts. . . .

Bring your attention back to your trunk, where you center into the perfect balance of strength and flexibility that helps sustain you through the storms that blow through this grove from time to time. . . .

Retain this sense of perfect balance as you step out from your tree, back into your human form. Thoth is there with you, to share your experience. Notice that your tree friend seems healthier and more vital from your encounter in this way. You may wish to leave a gift for your tree before you return. . . .

Thoth will guide you back into your body through your crown. Be sure to take a few grounding breaths to assure that you are fully connected with and centered in your physical form before opening your eyes. . . .

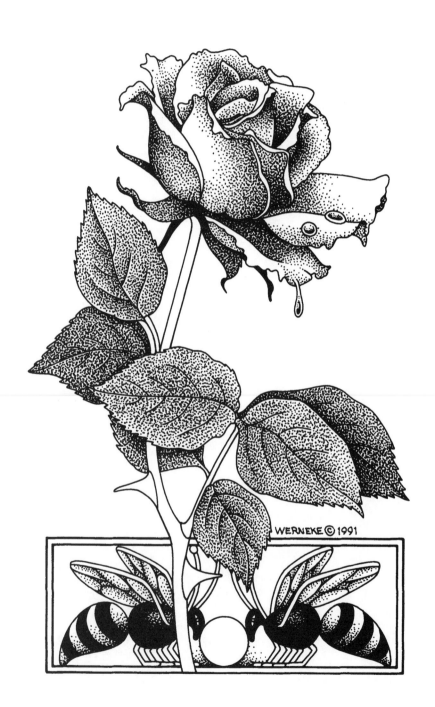

WERNEKE © 1991

ROSE
Perfection of Self/Opening of Heart

Undisputed queen of all flowers, the rose is unparalleled in beauty, useful in medicine, and cherished for its scent and delicate flavor. In medieval times, rosaries were made from compressed rose petals.

Less common is the rose's association with death. Cemeteries in Switzerland are sometimes called rose gardens, symbolizing not only death but rebirth and resurrection. In ancient Rome, tombs were decked and graves planted with roses.

The term *sub rosa* dates back to the Romans, Greeks, and Persians, who placed roses above the door at council meetings as a sign of secrecy and silence.

The rose has often been associated with the heart and its essence equated with love. These are the aspects addressed in the Cauldron, for it is important to each person's development to have and maintain an open heart. This journey is meant to fulfill the need in every person to recognize his or her own beauty and perfection.

Those who journey with the rose will have an opportunity to experience the opening of their hearts as the petals unfurl to reveal the essence of rose, the essence of love.

Rose Journey

[*This journey has a different alchemy, so proceed with the journey as follows.*]

Ground and center with your breath and generate lots of love to your heart flame to make it strong and bright for the alchemy. . . . Take note of your crown as the doorway to your consciousness. Be sure your

Cauldron is gold and the liquid inside it is pink. When you stir the pink water in the Golden Cauldron, it rises to meet the flame in your heart. As the water is converted to steam, it creates a fountain of pink mist. Let your consciousness rise up within the steam and fountain out your crown. . . . You are engulfed in a pink mist. You are aware of the presence of Thoth, even if you can't see him in the pink fog. Feel the softness of the pink mist and enjoy its embrace. . . .

Out of the pink mist emerges a rosebud. It might be on a single stem or part of a bush. There are glossy green leaves on strong, graceful stems. Sharp thorns give off an aura of protection.

Sunlight penetrates the pink mist, glistening on the drops of dew caught in the folds of the leaves and blossom, and as the warm rays of the sun burn off the fog, the petals of the rose slowly begin to open. There is a direct connection between this rose and your heart, and as each petal unfolds you can feel the opening of your heart. . . . [*Pause.*]

As this superb rose blossom continues to open, it emits the most exquisite fragrance, generating feelings of perfection, beauty, and love. . . .

Take a moment to honor the beauty and perfection of this rose. . . . As you breathe deeply, inhaling the fragrance of the rose, allow its essence to permeate to the core of your being. . . .

A blending occurs and you merge with and experience what it is like to be the rose. . . . Feel the sensuality of the sunlight on your open petals. Notice the sensation of the breeze caressing your body, touching every cell. You are filled with the love that you feel for the rose. All of your senses are heightened, and you become aware that you are in a garden. Your sense of hearing is increased to amplify the teeming life of this garden. There is an incessant hum that differentiates into the sound of a honeybee that visits you, entering through the open heart of your outstretched petals, dancing as it gathers sweet pollen. . . . Receive a message from this partner in the continuing dance of life. There is a teaching here about ecstasy and your inner beauty. . . . [*Pause.*]

Let your attention be drawn from the blossom downward to the root system of your rosebush. Your roots are strong and reach deeply into the soil, holding you securely in the place from which is drawn your nourishment. Notice your connection to the earth and become aware of yourself as grounded, even with the joy and ecstasy of your experience. . . .

Become aware of the presence of Thoth. He assists you back into your ordinary consciousness through a gradual transformation that allows you to bring your feelings of perfection and beauty into your physical form. As you exchange the body of the rose for your human body, you maintain normal size and the rose becomes small, concentrated to fit within your heart center, where it continues to radiate its exquisite fragrance.

[*Be sure to ground and center in your physical body. . . .*]

WERNEKE © 1991

EAGLE
Making Choices

Eagle is a powerful symbol of nobility and discrimination. To Native Americans, he represents the highest expression of spirit. Eagle feathers have intrinsic value. They symbolize truth and are considered sacred, reserved for use in many forms of healing and ceremony. To have Eagle as an ally is to have the benefit of his expanded capacity for discernment.

In the Golden Cauldron, Eagle clarifies choices. As you soar with him, you can view your choices and make decisions about your life based on the keen vision and lofty perspective you have as Eagle.

Whenever you see wings as a symbol, as in the winged disk of Egypt or the logo of the Cauldron, they represent our High Self, our parent overself that is perfectly balanced (it takes two wings to fly) and beyond attachment to our physical bodies. Our High Self provides us with a collective overview, like the expanded perspective of Eagle. Through Eagle's eyes, we perceive our world from a much more clear-sighted viewpoint.

In this journey, Eagle helps you choose your goals rather than achieve them. If you're having trouble deciding on a goal or have an array of choices, Eagle gives momentum in establishing what is right for you and setting other possibilities aside. Eagle also provides a view from your High Self of any situation in your life that needs scrutiny.

The eagle I most often use is a fishing eagle, which flies high over a big river with ample and diverse fish. He picks the one he will eat and then tucks in his wings and dives, grabbing hold of his choice. Or Eagle might show you different possibilities for the resolution of the situation you have chosen.

Eagle hovers in the air while viewing his options. From this vantage point, he goes for his choice whole-heartedly. All choices are equal, in the sense that whichever is picked is enjoyed for as much as it is worth. If you want more, don't denigrate the previous choice. Be content with the choice you have made so as not to hinder your development. You can always return another time to try a new choice.

It is often helpful to follow this journey with a visit with Elephant, who can help you bring whatever choice you have made into physical manifestation.

Eagle Journey

[*Do the alchemy. . . .*]

In order to take a ride with Eagle, you must go to his house. Thoth points to a high cliff, on the side of which there is a big aerie in the crotch of an old snag tree. You must climb the craggy cliff and find footing on one of the limbs that hold the nest in place. There is a magnificent adult eagle inside the nest. As you look into his eyes, inwardly express your desire, from your heart, for whatever you wish to look at or make a request about your goal for this experience. Tell the eagle that you wish to make a decision and need help discerning from the choices that are available. Be willing to be surprised. . . .

As you stand on the branch that holds the nest, begin your transformation into an eagle. Your feet start to shift into talons that grip the branch better. You have tail feathers that stick out to help you maintain balance. Gradually you feel more comfortable as you take on the shape of an eagle. From your shoulders down through your arms, lift up first one great eagle wing, stretching and feeling the big feathers unfurl. . . . Then open your other wing, fanning it out and drawing it back in close. Preen your feathers, nestling your new beak in the down of your chest. Fluff up the feathers on your back and shoulders, and feel the pin feathers on top of your head. During this metamorphosis, experience all stages of development, from a fledgling to a full-grown eagle.

Look down from your perch at the river below, so far down that it looks like a string, a tiny ribbon. There is nothing between you and that river. A light wind ruffles your feathers, rocking you gently. As you slowly unfold your wings, reach out in both directions and let them fan out, slowly. . . . The same breeze now has more lift; you must grip the branch to keep from lifting off. Release your talons and let the breeze lift you. It will take a moment to feel comfortable in the air, yet very quickly you catch the wind and begin to soar, exalting in the freedom of flight. . . .

The eagle that is in the nest takes off and spends a few moments teaching you the art and joy of flying. Let concerns and worries fall away in the face of greater horizons as the vista spreads before you. Follow your eagle partner as he heads toward the far horizon. . . .

Pay attention to the ground beneath you. Notice the terrain, the time of day, and the direction in which you fly. . . .

Take five deep breaths and hold the last one or breathe very slowly as you and your eagle friend arrive at your destination. . . .

Your eagle partner gives a loud cry. Your ears ring as the sound resonates throughout your body. Hold your breath for as long as you can while you remain poised in midair, fluttering, hovering. . . . Blow out the air through your mouth slowly, and then look down. The ground seems far away, yet with your eagle eyes you can see quite clearly. Take slow, long breaths as you look at the distant landscape. . . .

As Eagle, you have telescopic vision through which you can perceive objects or symbols that represent your situation or the choices you wish to make. There might be a variety of options. Use all of your senses to evaluate the alternatives that are presented. Eagle vision is discriminating; you can feel with this sight and gain insight into which of your choices will engender the appropriate future.

As you continue to hover, look for the choice that feels right, that brings you joy or contentment. When you discover one that you are interested in trying, hold it in your mind. Focus all your attention on it and take five deep, strong breaths. . . .

On your last exhale, dive. Feel yourself dropping through space faster than you could have imagined. Feel the wind tear at you as you swoop down with all the speed and majesty of Eagle. Grasp the symbol you have chosen with your talons and clutch it to your heart. As you fly back up into the air holding the symbol to your chest, let it merge with your heart and become one with it.

As you fly back to your nest, you are flying into your chosen future. Pay attention to the changes you can perceive in the landscape below.

Notice as many things as you can while you maintain the sight of Eagle. As you follow your eagle friend, it is clear that your choice brings you contentment and strength, and you are at peace.

The eagle returns to the nest with his meal and eats at home, sharing the food with his family. You may wish to make a spiritual offering of food to help sustain these eagles.

Receive any further message from your eagle friend. . . .

As you stand perched on the branch outside the nest, you metamorphose back into your human form. . . . As you climb down from the nest, your perceptions are more expansive, and you retain the peaceful feeling you have gained about what you've chosen or what has been revealed to you. When you return to the path where Thoth is waiting, consult with him about any further questions you might have about this experience or your situation.

[*Thoth assists you back into your body.* . . .]

WERNEKE © 1991

ELEPHANT
Manifesting Goals/Problem Solving

All things on this planet, all physical forms, are born of the element earth; that's why we call Earth our mother. The massive elephant is the most earthy of animals and understands the manifestation process as does no other. Elephants' capacity to manifest is connected to following the path of the heart, and elephants have huge hearts. The journey with Elephant teaches us how to manifest what we want or need in the physical world.

The Hindus have a deity named Ganesha, who is the son of Shiva. It is Ganesha who has brought Elephant into the Cauldron. This being has a royal intelligence, and when you come into his presence, he shares your burdens and helps you find the path through your obstacles. As Lord of Solutions, he brings peace and tranquillity. When you have a great task, call on Ganesha and he will help you attain the resolve to intellectually get going—to take each step and to see ahead with your intellect. He will help you find resolution for your troubles. You can use this journey with Ganesha to help you manifest your goals and solve problems.

It is best to have a specific purpose when you take this journey. Choose a goal or an obstacle to work with. Ganesha, in his elephant form, can also help you manifest the things you need in your life. You can choose to focus on immediate or long-range plans. It is through the realizations of your wants, needs, and desires that you will be able to see into the future, unencumbered by hopes and concerns of the present. Learn from Elephant how to get what you want and then look to see what lies beyond your expectations. It is possible to see into the future and from there look back on the questions of today with a broader perspective and the wisdom of hindsight.

This journey has two parts. The first part helps you see immediate steps you need to take, and the second helps you get a clear view of your ultimate goal. With Elephant, you love and celebrate the earth on which you stand.

Elephant Journey

[*Do the Cauldron alchemy. . . .*]

Thoth points the way to a night scene in India. It's dark. First see an elephant's eyes—big, intelligent, and willing to share your burden. As you look into the eyes of your elephant, tell him your problem or what you would like to accomplish. . . . His form comes into view, and you become aware of the night sky, with a full moon and a blanket of stars, and then of the earth. You hear in the distance the music of hand cymbals and dancing feet.

You have entered the realm of Ganesha, the elephant god, where all your burdens become light. The elephant drops slowly to one knee, and you climb onto his back. Sit in comfort, arms out to your sides, thumbs covering index fingernails, chest forward, head back.

The elephant begins to take you on a walk through nature. Imagine his head coming from your chest as you sway from side to side in a figure eight, an infinity pattern. . . . Ride the elephant through the thickest of bushes, forests, or jungle, aware that no obstacles thwart your passage. Pay attention, for the elephant is showing you how to take each step as you continue to sway. . . .

You are following your heart's desire and allowing your intellect to help you find the correct, balanced path. As you sway with the motion of the elephant, chest forward, you feel the elephant's heart as your own, and your heart merges with his and naturally begins to open. . . .

The terrain grows steeper, and the path more rigorous and narrow. Still the elephant continues, step after step. Receive an intellectual awareness of what your problem or situation is and what you can do about it. Notice that it is connected to following your heart—being centered and at peace within your heart. . . .

Dawn is breaking, and at first light you begin to get a sense of the immediate steps you must take to clear the problem or achieve your goals. As you sway with the elephant, he clears your path. By the time you've reached the top of the mountain, your heart is fully open. You've merged with, become one with, the elephant.

From your new vantage point on the peak of the mountain, look with elephant eyes across the new horizon. You have stopped swaying. Feel your love for Mother Earth as you look toward the sunrise. The first ray of sunlight appears and *strikes your third eye.* Allow yourself to experience the full impact and intensity of the sunlight as it penetrates your third eye during the time it takes for the sun to rise. . . .

Extend your chest and open your arms wide with your palms up. As the horizon opens out before you, take five deep breaths. Throw your head and trunk back with each inhale through your nose, and blow out the breath from your mouth as you bring your head forward. . . .

At the end of the fifth breath, either drop forward with your third eye to the floor or lie on your back. Keep still. With your final exhale, begin to float and allow whatever will to happen. As you take off, relax and enjoy whatever comes up. Allow your vision to carry you into the future. The elephant has cleared your path and shown you the way. You now have a chance to explore. Fly into the horizon. Look beyond your expectations. Stay as long as you are comfortable. . . . [*Long pause.*]

To come back, think of the elephant's eyes. He will be there sitting on the mountaintop, and you are sitting in his lap, between his legs, which become pillars of your own personal temple. . . .

For your gift to the elephant, you might wish to offer a prayer or blessing for the healing of some problem on Earth. . . .

As you return down the path in the light of the new day, there are no obstacles. Thoth meets you on the way and spends a moment with you, sharing your experience. . . .

[*Thoth shows you back to your body through your crown. Remember to use the grounding breath and be sure you are fully centered and connected with your physical form before opening your eyes. . . .*]

WERNEKE © 1991

POISON OAK
Protection

Poison oak often grows in areas that have been disturbed. It naturally creates a place of protection that allows the earth around it to heal. Those who are not respectful and cautious in its presence may pay dire consequences.

Poison oak is repellent to many people, and for good reason. Anyone who has suffered from its miserable effects knows great respect for this plant. This journey is not meant to be a cure for those allergic to poison oak. Rather, it can help you in adapting to and gaining control of your world.

In the Cauldron, Poison oak offers personal self-protection for sensitive and gentle people. Once you have taken this journey, you can move through it very quickly to generate an aura of power and respect.

Poison Oak Journey

[*Go through the alchemy to Thoth. . . .*]
As Thoth guides you through a curtain or doorway, you transform instantly into a seed. It's as though you have been lifted by a gentle breeze, swirling lightly, and when you enter a pocket of stillness, you fall, the force of your weight planting you in the ground. . . .

Your seed-self is enveloped in dark, damp coolness. Moisture permeates the earthborn seed, and you can feel the changes as you become a gnarl, then a burl, and soon start pushing out roots that reach down into the earth. With the weight and energy of your roots reaching down, your crown is pushed up and your body rises, slowly curling and twirling, spinning clockwise around anything that's in your way, grow-ing upward. It's winter, and your growth is slow enough to feel the starkness of dormancy, even as you grow larger. You are aware of yourself as brown and barkish and brittle, and with very little green, even as you continue to grow.

Notice the warmth of the sun on your branches, and allow yourself to feel the potent juices begin to rise up through your roots and spread upward through the trunk of your body. Although your form seems somewhat thin and scrawny, you feel the sap pushing up and out to the extremes of your exterior, putting pressure against your bark. As the poison rushes outward, your chakras begin to open. It is now spring-time, and you feel yourself burst into new greening. The sap, water, and light feed this accelerated urge to blossom. The new growth that is awakened is full and green and soft, in sharp contrast to your body, which is barky, hard, and sparse. You have become full and lush and vigorous. . . .

You are aware of the energy within the earth feeding your interior structure, as the potent juices flow densely into the ends of your leaves, which become so full that they curl. Your leaves shine and vibrate with the force of the summer sun. They become tinged with red, and the sap that flows through feels like blood. The red color in your leaves is dense, like garnets, and becomes so thick as it builds that power inherent in the juices comes into its own and starts radiating out and around you. . . .

A feeling of empowerment encompasses your domain, for the potent juices bring instant vitality and create the knowledge that your energy is whole, radiating a kind of shield that cannot be penetrated. . . . Enjoy the sense of protection from this force field that surrounds you. . . .

You have an opportunity to commune with the spirit of Poison Oak and are given a special teaching about protection and shielding. . . . [*Long pause.*]

The season is now fall, and it's time to complete the cycle and return. The magic is dispersed into the air as energy and into seeds of the berries that fall to the ground. Put your consciousness into one of the berries. It feels like both the end and the beginning as you release yourself and fall back into your body.

Thoth is there to discuss this experience with you. . . .

[*Thoth will assist you back into your body. . . .*]

PART III

JOURNEYS FOR AWAKENING

These journeys awaken your potential for expanded awareness, opening doorways to let new understanding enter your consciousness. Relish these moments, and continue to practice these journeys as meditations to catalyze further action and growth in your life.

WERNEKE © 1991

HIPPOPOTAMUS
Rebirth

Hippopotamus is the midwife in the Cauldron. In Egypt, she is the goddess Tarät (Taueret), who attends each and every birth. She is seen on the walls of the temples assisting at the birth of the sun each morning after it has completed its journey through the underworld.

There were three couches in the tomb of Tutankhamen. The first was the hippopotamus couch, which symbolizes birthing into physical form. The second was the cow couch, which corresponds to accessing the astral plane. Third was the lion couch, which has to do with birthing the stellar body.

Talismans of Tarät were carried for fertility and during the birthing process as well. Although classical Egyptology interpretations often show her as a vanquished villain of darkness, I have always found her to be compassionate, sensual, and full of wonderful wisdom and guidance.

Hippos have disappeared from Egypt, where they used to flourish along the Nile among the also-vanished lotus. They were slaughtered for their teeth, which are prized for ivory that does not yellow with age. Hippo skins are extremely thick, although quite sensitive to the sun. According to one source, a hippo hide takes six years to tan by hand. The resulting leather is so hard that it can cut a diamond. Perhaps that's why in Mesopotamia hippo hides were used to make chastity belts!

Sometimes hippos appear blue, and they were often expressed that way in Egyptian art. They secrete a bluish purple, reddish liquid somewhat like our sweat if they are kept from their pools for too long.

Hippos give birth in the water in places where they feel absolutely safe. They must live where the river is shallow and the current slow, for they are not great swimmers, and a swift current can carry them to their deaths.

When you journey through the Cauldron to visit Tarät, you have an opportunity to reexperience your physical birth in the presence of a midwife capable of holding a safe and secure place for what may have been a traumatic event in your life. Once you have resolved your birth trauma, you might have a variety of new experiences with this journey. Sometimes you can experience birth in a past or parallel life, or Tarät may teach you how to be born in ecstasy and joy, free from the pain that is most always associated with the birthing process. Each time you visit Tarät, you will be nourished with the milk of wisdom, the pearl of great price, as you enter life anew.

Hippopotamus Journey

[*Do the alchemy. . . .*]

Because you are traveling to the Nile, Thoth may transform into an ibis to take you to his homeland. It is that quiet, magical time between night and day, just before the first light of dawn illuminates the eastern horizon. You are brought to a path near the river. The drumbeats you hear are the heartbeat of Mother Earth. Warm and moist, the balmy air wraps around you in a soft embrace. You can feel the moisture from the dew that has gathered on the grass along the path. You come to a place where two flamingos guard the passageway to the river. The surrounding mountains are blanketed with deep, lush, velvetlike terrain tinged with the same pink color as the flamingos.

Thoth leads you along the path to the great River of Life, where the papyrus grows along the banks and hippos can faintly be seen luxuriating among the lotus flowers, nibbling lush greens in the pale, early morning light. You are directed to one of the lovely lotus blossoms for your vantage point. There is just a hint of the hidden fragrance that this flower will exude when the sun shines forth to open its heavenly crown. Feel the strength and beauty of this exquisite flower.

It is warm and peaceful here. As you look out over the river, you can barely make out the silhouettes of some hippo heads with their gleaming eyes in the semidarkness.

To get a closer look, you must follow the stem of the lotus down into the water, down to the rhizomes, the horizontal roots beneath the surface. The water is warm, and you will find that in this dimension breathing comes easily, even under the water. There is a heartbeat that is creating some kind of vibration in the water. You sense the presence of the hippos and realize that the vibration is created by their heartbeats, conducted by the water. They have huge hearts.

Feel yourself connect to one of the hippos. Make eye contact and request her assistance as your midwife in this birthing experience. . . .

In order to explore and reexperience your physical birth, you must travel further down the root of your lotus, following these deeper shoots as they descend into the rich mud of the river bottom, taking you back through time, back through your childhood, back to your earliest memories, and further—back to the very source of your life. . . .

You are in your mother's womb—safe, secure, gently rocked and enveloped by the amniotic fluid. There is the ever-present beating of your mother's heart. As long as the heartbeat is there you know you are safe, for the heartbeat is the rhythm of life. . . . [*Pause to get the feel of the womb.*]

You begin to experience a sense of striving to be born, striving to come forth into the light of life on Earth. Be aware, as the striving awakens within you, that you are choosing to be born. And now, as you reexperience your birth, do so with the full awareness and acceptance that you have chosen this life. . . . [*Pause.*]

As you come forth into the light of new life, and while observing your life from birth to the present, you have an opportunity to forgive others who may have caused you anguish or pain. In those places where you would judge yourself, forgive yourself. Accept that you are a beautiful, unique, wonderful being. It is through forgiveness that you can resolve the past traumas of your life. . . . [*Pause to complete instruction.*]

As you move back up through time, back up through the lotus, you will find yourself once again cradled in the exquisite lotus blossom. Its soft color and delicious fragrance generate a feeling of well-being as you rock in the gentle current of the river, presently watching the hippos as they feed and play in the early morning calm. . . .

Now that you've experienced your birth, enjoy the feeling and look toward beginning anew. . . .

The lotus releases its roots, and the current of the river gently and purposefully carries you downstream. With wonder, you begin to anticipate the nourishment of life and love. . . .

The river widens into a bay. Here, in the slower current, you see Tarät, your hippo midwife, once again. She beckons, and you dive off the lotus and swim toward her. . . . Tarät opens her mouth and there, on her tongue, is a beautiful, luminescent pearl. She gives this pearl to you. . . . You may swallow it or place it inside yourself. As you absorb this pearl, feel its nourishment and luminosity spread throughout your being. . . .

You can ride on Tarät's back as she swims slowly to the shore. She may even be wearing a necklace that you can hold on to. . . .

When Tarät lets you off at the water's edge, take a moment to receive any further message or instructions she might have for you at this time. . . .

You may choose to give her a gift. . . .

Thoth is there. Take a moment to share your experience with him. . . .

[Thoth will assist you back into your body. Be sure to ground and center. . . .]

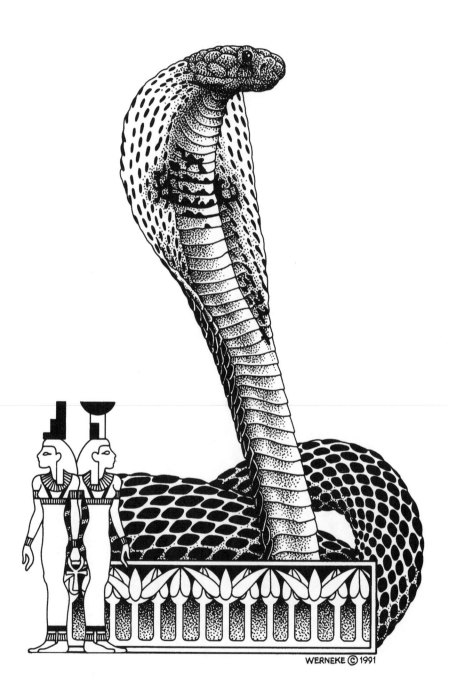

WERNEKE © 1991

Cobra
Awakening of Energy

Cobra is a personification of a force, an intelligence. In Egypt she was called Buto or Uatchet (also Udjat). Uatchet means "the awakener." Cobras represent the highest form of serpent energy and wisdom in Egypt. You will see Cobra on the crown of Pharaoh representing Lower Egypt and the Low, or Hidden, Self, which is the subconscious or unconscious mind.

The uraeus crown, a circlet of gold with a cobra at the third eye, is a mystical symbol indicating that the wearer has been through the snake initiation and is an awakened being. Some crowns have two snakes on them. This signifies a further initiation balancing the two polarized halves of the energy of the one snake. When worn on the head of Pharaoh, the uraeus was said to spit fire at the eyes of his enemies.

In Egypt, Uatchet, as the uraeus snake, was the hieroglyph for "goddess," and "Uraeus" later became one of the more popular secret names of God listed in ancient papyri and medieval texts. The birth and death goddesses, Isis and Nephthys, were identified with the dual serpent, mother of life and afterlife. Only they could help the soul through the section of the underworld inhabited by serpent deities.

As a healing ally, Cobra is powerful and indispensable. She has the capacity to devour diseases by eating tumors and other virulent pathogens, because serpent systems are not vulnerable to the same diseases as ours. As you develop your relationship with this new ally, ask when it is appropriate to utilize her power in this way. It is also interesting to note that cobra venom, although poisonous, is useful in many kinds of medicine.

When it is time to offer a gift to Cobra, you have an opportunity to give her something that no longer serves you, something that you don't want, like a disease or a negative habit pattern. Make sure you choose something that Cobra is willing to devour at the time.

The first time you take this journey, the kundalini, historically represented by a sleeping serpent coiled at the base of the spine, is awakened and raised. As a result, the tap to the spinal current of energy is opened, enabling you to access the universal life-force energy for healing. Your heart is connected to your High Self as Cobra forges a direct channel between your heart and cosmic consciousness.

There are traditional elements of fear surrounding the awakening of kundalini energy. Some of us fear the lack of control experienced when this strong energy rises without proper preparation of our minds and/or bodies. Cobra catalyzes the increment of opening and expansion that is in accordance with the preparedness of each individual who comes to her for this initiation.

It is important to be aware that some initiations are not appropriate for all people at all times, so if you have an intuitive flash to wait, you should listen. You will know when the time is right—when you are in a state of psychological and physical readiness.

The snake is the center of your life force, just as the river Nile is the spinal current of the planet. This awakening is not something new that you are gaining but some intrinsic part that you are becoming aware of and can begin to utilize. The channel that is opened in your spine expands with use. It causes the strengthening and enlarging of all the chakras and the auric system. They all become brighter and larger. By your intention, you can access the awakened energy in your hands for healing. The more you direct it in that way, the stronger it becomes.

It is optimum to fast for twenty-four hours before you experience Cobra for the first time. If you do not have an opportunity to fast, drink lots of water during the prior twenty-four hours, and try to avoid journeying right after a meal.

This Cobra initiation takes strength and endurance. Once you have experienced this journey, you can practice it as a meditation whenever it feels appropriate.

The Cobra will always be with you!

Cobra Journey

[Sit cross-legged if you can, crossing your arms over your chest at the wrists, with your right band over your heart chakra. Keep your spine as straight as possible. I will call this snake "she," because the one I work with is definitely a female.

Use the alchemy to get to Thoth. . . .

Thoth will help you back into your body, still in an altered, light-body state, so that you can experience this initiation from within your physical form and with all your body sensitivities. . . .]

Cobra approaches from the rear. She is first heard as she hisses. Your body tingles as it becomes aware of the presence of the snake. . . .

Welcome Cobra. . . . You can feel the resonance in your spine as she slithers across the floor. This cobra is very large, possibly as much as four inches in diameter and fifteen to twenty feet long. She turns to the right side of your body, climbs up over your right leg, and moves on across your lap to your left leg. Make eye contact as she passes in front of you. *Feel* the sensation as the cobra crawls over your skin—she is extremely sensuous. Notice the mark on her head when her hood is fanned, as it is throughout this journey.

As Cobra winds around, she touches back to the floor behind you. When you feel her approach your first chakra center at the base of your spine, tighten your sphincter muscles just for a second. As you release the muscles, Cobra bites into your first chakra center, her fangs reaching down into and through your root, as though they're reaching all the way into the earth. The sensation is as if the bottom of your body opens up and almost disintegrates into Earth, connecting you to all her power. Earth welcomes you. You are open to her, and you feel yourself merge with her. It is as though you are completely surrounded by and composted into Earth. As you break apart and disintegrate, the deeper knowledge of the element of earth is absorbed into you through this melding process. . . . *[Long pause.]*

This connection seems endless, and the snake proceeds on to wind herself around the right side of your body once more, creating a coil. . . .

When she reaches your spine again, she is behind you in the area of your second center, your genital chakra. Here Cobra seems to divide into two bodies, with two heads. There is a sudden sensation of being under water as one of the cobras enters your second chakra and passes straight through your body, her head stopping at your lap area. During your immersion in the water, you are dissolved and can experience the deepest knowledge and intelligence of water flowing, being infused into every aspect of your being. . . . There is a deep level of comprehension of fluidity, emotions, compassion, and psychic sensitivity. . . . [*Long pause.*]

Excess water disappears into the mouth of the snake that's in your lap. She draws back into your belly and out of your lower back through your second chakra, then joins with her other head and proceeds as one cobra again. . . .

Cobra continues to coil around your body, winding around on top of herself. As she comes around to your back again, she is at the level of your third chakra center, higher up, at your solar plexus area. She hisses. You feel the vibration and resonance of her hiss throughout your body, particularly up and down your spine. . . .

Cobra bites again. This time it feels hot. The feeling of heat grows and becomes brilliant as it burns right through your body and out the front of your solar plexus. It pours out like a great spiritual fire, spreading and emanating, projecting the essence of fire from your center of personal will and power. It is very brilliant and very hot. It feels as though you are being completely consumed by the burning heat of this spiritual fire. As you are burned away, the knowledge of fire enters through your spirit. . . . As your body is reconstructed from its own ashes, it contains more complete knowledge of the element fire. . . . [*Long pause.*]

Cobra continues to wind around your body. When she comes around again and crosses your back, she passes over your heart chakra and continues making her coil. As she approaches your front again, she opens her mouth and proceeds to swallow your hands, your wrists, and your heart. And she just keeps going around your body, spiraling up higher. As she proceeds, you might notice a feeling of loneliness, a sense of longing and searching. Simply acknowledge your feelings as the cobra continues.

When she gets behind you once more, she is at your neck chakra. Cobra bites again. Here you get a sense of the vapors, the fire and water combined to create steam and mist. Air swirls about you, and you may feel some giddiness or lightheadedness. Your mind expands as the winds blow freely throughout your being, whipping you to pieces and scattering them to the farthest reaches of the four directions. Each particle is now combined with a sense of unity and communion, and you are taught the deeper meanings of the element of air. . . . [*Long pause.*]

Cobra enters through the back of your neck where she bit you and works her way up into your head. When she reaches the upper middle area inside your brain, she spits out of her mouth a crystal in the shape of the mark on her forehead. It is planted there, superimposed over the pineal gland.

Cobra continues moving up through the inside of your head and comes out your third eye. Notice the sensation in your third eye as it is being enlarged by the fanned head of Cobra. Once her head is out, she circles to the left around the top of your head and forms the uraeus crown by returning to your third eye, dipping down, and rearing up again facing forward.

When Cobra is in this final position, she hisses. You can hear the hissing, feeling it as a vibration of deep sound within your ears, as though you are hearing cymbals or a high-pitched sound inside your ears. As the hissing continues, the top of your crown feels a moving, tickling, vibrating sensation, within which you experience your crown chakra opening. . . .

The crystal Cobra planted begins to glow and sparkle inside your head, creating a lot of light. Turn your eyes upward and inward, focusing on the top of the back of your head. There are nine cobras there, full blown and creating the image of a fan above and behind you.

Your heart chakra is wide open. A strong link is apparent between your heart and crown chakras, generating feelings of intense love and a connection with all of life and the cosmos. Herein is the understanding between heart and High Self. Cobra continues to hiss throughout this blissful state. The sensation in your body is one of great love, warmth, and unification with the entire universe. You are filled with a sense of completeness as the snake continues to hiss. Hold to your highest ideas of wisdom and love during this extended state. Notice any visions, shapes, and colors that arise. . . . [*Long pause.*]

When this attunement is complete, Cobra stops hissing. She begins to unwind and slips back into your head and out the back of your neck as she slowly uncoils herself from your body, slithering along your skin. Notice how sensual this feels.

When she has completely unwound herself, she will come around to the front of you and rear up to face you directly, eye to eye. You may wish to make an offering and can choose something that you no longer want, such as a habit you have wanted to give up, a characteristic that no longer serves you, or something negative that she is willing to devour. Ask her first if your choice is appropriate. . . .

Cobra has a further message for you, and you may have questions for her. Take the time you need to get to know this powerful ally.

Discuss your experience with Thoth. . . .

[*Thoth will tap you on your crown to bring you back into your ordinary consciousness. Be sure to ground and center. . . . You can redirect any excess energy so that it comes out the palms of your hands.*]

WERNEKE © 1991

Stag

Initiation into Ley Lines

This journey is an initiation, and it is dedicated to the Goddess, for Stag serves the Goddess. As her consort, he supports all those who work with her. He is positive male energy, a powerful ally who provides a great experience of what true male energy can be. This initiation has the effect of nurturing your third chakra, the center of your personal will and power.

In this journey, you will encounter the shape-shifting face of a stag/man, one of the earliest representations of the "Horned God," who was a consort of the Goddess. The stag represents the male energy that is in all of us and helps us manifest what we need in this world. He is frequently considered a source of fertility and power. The treelike appearance of his horns may also designate association with the spirits of the forest.

Through Stag, you will be introduced to ley lines. These are the pathways that form the meridian system of the planet, the lines of force within the field of Earth's surface through which energy passes. Most of the power places of the world are erected where ley lines intersect. Stonehenge is an obvious example, as is the Great Pyramid. As you become conscious of ley lines, you gain awareness of polarity and flows within our ecological system, and you can align your personal energies to work with those of Earth. You can travel along these lines to visit any of the power centers of the planet.

The grid system that is created from the ley lines is part of the integrity of the earth. One of the dangers of industrial technology is that some mining and drilling practices create imbalances in the grid, resulting in alterations and blockages in Earth's energy flows.

When journeying with Stag, you have the opportunity to bring balance and energetic vitality to the meridian system of your own body, which is a reflection of the ley-line system of Earth.

Stag Journey

[*Do the alchemy.* . . .]

Thoth is standing in the mist, with a raven sitting on his shoulder. The bird flies to your shoulder, and you feel its weight and notice the shiny black of its feathers.

There is a path coming out of the mist that opens before your feet. As you follow it, you come upon a rectangular portal or doorway. Step through and walk down into a circle of large stones. Some are fallen and cracked and others are still upright, although extremely weathered. In the center of the circle is a flat slab that has a circle drawn on it. The raven flies from your shoulder and alights on a stone. It looks at you with an intense, unblinking gaze and asks if you are ready and willing to undergo this initiation, which will be for the interconnection of the grids of the world, the ley lines, with those of your body, your meridians or *chi* lines.

If your heart answers *yes,* relax and lie face up on the stone. (If it says *no,* go back and wait to take this journey until it feels right. Take time to talk to Thoth.) The raven moves out of the way so you can lie on the circle. You sense and now feel the presence of someone standing behind you. . . .

There is a slight pressure or touch on your throat as a piece of a stag's horn, carved like a knife, is drawn across it. You find yourself looking up into the face of a compassionate man. He is an archetype of the male energy that serves the Goddess. As you watch his face, it changes from that of an incredibly wise, knowing, and caring man into the primal, unknowable, animal face of the stag.

He helps you rise and shows you the circle again. All the stones are now upright. Take a moment to experience the energy flows in your own body. . . . [*Pause.*] Look beyond the stones and feel how the energy is vibrating out along the lines, healing the land and its people. . . . [*Pause.*]

Stag blesses you for your commitment and then takes you on another journey, traveling along the ley lines to a particular place of power. It may be a temple or a special natural configuration. The two of you go deeply into this journey, which is into yourselves, where you see the reflection of Earth's meridian system in your own body. The raven is with you and the stag. . . . [*Long pause.*]

Thoth joins you when it's time. Discuss your experience with him before returning to your body. . . . [*Be sure to ground and center. . . .*]

WERNEKE ©1991

WHALE
Sonic Initiation

The whale has been regarded as a powerful totem animal by native Pacific coastal tribes. Its teeth and bones are considered potent amulets, conferring some of the physical powers of Whale on their owners, including the ability to overturn the canoes of enemies.

Many species of whales are facing extinction because of relentless hunting for their meat and oil. Once-numerous populations are swiftly diminishing, and it is not known how much effect pollution of the oceans is having on the immune systems of these extremely sensitive and gentle mammals.

Water carries *sound* much better than it carries *light,* and whales can see with their ears. Before the oceans became polluted with the sound of propellers and engines, whales could communicate with one another across great expanses. Some scientists have suggested that when whales beach themselves, it is because their echo-location systems are functioning improperly, causing them to be confused about where they are.

The whale that brought this journey into the Cauldron is the humpback whale, although all of the many species of whales are keepers of the records of the development of Earth. They are like sounding boards, singing the tale of our Mother Earth out into the universe. This journey tunes you to the song of the spheres, the vibration of the whales that endlessly emanates our planetary tonal signature. When you are initiated, the song is encoded inside you and will continue to resonate in accordance with your attention. It can work like a sonic filter for your consciousness, cleaning, clearing, and making space for expanded awareness.

This journey lends itself well to group work. Try sitting in a circle holding hands. At the appropriate moment, your group can sing a song back to the whales as your gift. The song will remain in the very center of your being. You thrum with it, vibrate with it, and it never leaves you.

It is helpful to listen to a tape of whale music before or during this journey.

Whale Journey

[*Do the alchemy. . . .*]

Thoth directs you to a sunny beach, where you walk across the sand toward the water. Listen to the sound of the waves as they break and roll up the shoreline. It's a beautiful, calm day, and it appears easy to swim out past the surf to where you can see the fountains spouting from the backs of the whales that are playing just off the coast. As soon as you enter the water and start swimming, you can hear their song. Mournful, high pitched, and deep, it enters through your heart and spreads throughout your body. Tune to it. . . .

One of the whales, a cow, makes eye contact with you and approaches you directly. She touches you with her tongue in greeting. There are several cows in the pod that you are swimming with, along with a few calves. They are huge, these leviathans of the deep. There is very direct communication between you and these whales that does not come through talking.

Hold on to your new whale friend or swim along in her slip, the place behind her fin where the babies swim, so that you are carried by the current she creates. She moves quite quickly considering her gargantuan size. Great care is taken to keep you safe, for a slap of her fin could result in death. She treats you with tenderness, as though you were her offspring. You learn to breathe with the whales, effortlessly, so that you may stay under the water with them for long periods of time.

The whales sing back and forth as they dive deeply, down to the depths of the ocean, where it's quite dark and full of sound. You are taken through a cave into a deep crevasse of the earth. It feels as though you have been swallowed and are inside the belly of the whale, but when you reach the bottom, you find yourself standing on white sand in a gigantic cavern under the world, at the bottom of the sea. Somehow it is lighter here, and you can see around you. Take a moment to ground into the place and feel the sand beneath your feet, between your toes. . . .

The whales are gone, but their song continues to echo throughout this resonant sound chamber. Their music moves through you like energy, penetrating to your core and entering your bones. There is no separation between you and the sound, for it is the beginning and end of everything. It is the intersection point in time where *now, then,* and *everywhere* come together. There is amazing healing power in this song, providing a way to connect with all consciousness. Notice how you can get folded up in it and come out at different places. Release yourself completely and get lost in the song. Even sight vanishes within this feeling. . . .

The vibrations of the song act like a trajectory and project you up and out of the ocean, away from Earth and out into deep space, to the farthest reaches of the cosmos that your consciousness can attain. There is no beginning or end to it. The tail of this song is a curve. . . . Let the infinite nature of the song seep into your understanding. . . .

Once you start vibrating to this sound, you understand your connection to the entire creation. This knowledge brings with it a great feeling of peace that can enhance your healing of yourself, each other, and the world. Once you vibrate with this song, it never leaves you. You are tuned, and you can always enter the song, for it is the song of the universe. . . .

Gradually your consciousness differentiates the sound of the waves on the water from the song. You are back on the beach, under a night sky filled with stars. The music is still there, and all sense of separation is gone. You can feel it right on your sternum, in the center of your being.

As you look out over the ocean, you can see the song in sparkling lights that emanate from the water. These light patterns of harmony feed the tectonic plates and go into crystalline structures. Experience the sound as *light* as well as sound. . . .

For your gift, sing back to Whale. . . .

Thoth is there. Recount your experience at this time. . . .

[*Thoth will assist you as you return to your ordinary consciousness, retaining the song in your soul.* . . .]

Swan

Inner Mate

In popular mythology, Swan represents the transformation from small, awkward, and ugly to large, graceful, and beautiful. He is regal and refined, a pure and royal emblem. Water, as a symbol of emotion, speaks of Swan's sensitivity and love, for swans live mostly in the water.

Swans figure in a wide range of historical and mythological references. From cultures as far apart as Siberia and Ireland, there is a shared belief that killing a swan brings misfortune or death. The Greek goddess of love, Aphrodite, has been depicted riding on a swan, and in Indonesia, the goddess Sarasvati is represented in the company of a swan. The most well-known transformation reference is probably to Zeus, king of the Greek gods, who turned himself into a swan to mate with earthly Leda.

Swans mate for life and understand connections that are generated from heart-to-heart contact. Swan comes into the Cauldron as an ally for finding your mate and for relationship counseling. The first time you enter the magical, idyllic realm of this journey, you will be introduced to your inner mate, that part of you that is your other side, or the balancing gender inside of you. If you are a woman, you have an internal man who brings balance to your femininity, and vice versa.

The true alchemical marriage is the merging of the masculine and feminine inside ourselves, and this journey instigates the courtship within which that marriage can occur. By working with Swan in this way, the optimum result can be the achievement of wholeness within one body. Once you have taken this journey and developed rapport with Swan, you can return and work on specific relationship issues. You will find that after you have become whole within yourself, relationships with others have more depth, and Swan can teach you how to attract your physical partner and mate.

The place to which you are taken in this journey is a sanctuary where you can stop being critical about yourself and stop having a sense of ugliness about yourself. Here you don't see the blemishes that ordinarily capture your attention. Instead, you appear and move with the grace of Swan, for you see yourself through the eyes of your beloved, who always looks at you with love.

Swan Journey

[*Do the Cauldron alchemy. . . .*]

Thoth will lead you to a beautiful lake or pond with swans swimming on its surface. It is a gorgeous spring day. There's a blue sky above with white puffy clouds and an idyllic landscape including weeping willows with their leaves resting on the water. As you approach, one of the swans moves toward you, checking you out. Imitate each of his moves— the curling of his neck, how he grooms himself. Make eye contact with this swan and feel for the heart connection. Just as water reflects the swan, you and the swan reflect each other. Ask for assistance with meeting and experiencing your inner mate through love.

Your transformation begins as you enter the water and turn into a swan. It feels wonderful. You are buoyed by your new feathers and glide effortlessly through the water with your strong, powerful legs and large, webbed feet, which are hidden beneath the surface. Take time to enjoy the feeling of being a swan, aware of your wings and your long, graceful neck. . . .

Your new swan friend takes off into flight and you follow, slowly circling the pond as you spiral upward, heading toward the puffy white clouds that stand out like giant marshmallows in the clear blue sky. You fly into and through the clouds, and as you come out the other side you know you have entered a magical space. Even the molecules in the air are tinged with color. Below you is a beautiful, magical land, and off in the distance you can see the turrets of a medieval castle or palace. It might be made of marble or crystal, with colorful pennants and flags atop its spires. There might even be a moat, and most certainly there is a pond or lake where you can land. Feel the beating of your heart as you descend, gliding down a rainbow to land on the water near the shore. . . .

As you step onto land, you are back in human form. Look into the water to see your reflection. You feel a vibrancy and joy, and the image that looks back at you is more beautiful or handsome than you could have imagined. Your body feels strong and vigorous, in perfect tone. You are clothed simply yet elegantly.

Listen for a moment to the melodic strains of a harp nearby. As you turn to follow the music, you become aware of the presence of someone you love. Feel this in your heart. Go and meet the one who waits for you. . . . Reach out and touch his or her face with your fingertips. . . . Spend the next few moments with this perfect inner mate. . . . [*Long pause.*]

You can return at any time to continue the relationship you have begun here. You may wish to exchange gifts. . . .

When it is time to leave this enchanting place, bid farewell and enter the water, transforming once again into the swan. With your swan friend, lift off and fly toward the clouds, circling this magical kingdom before passing back through the clouds and back to land on the original pond. When you step onto the shore, return to your human form. . . .

You might wish to give a gift to the swan who has been your guide. . . .

Thoth is with you now. Take time to discuss this work and future possibilities of working with Swan, your new friend and ally. . . .

[*Thoth assists you in returning into your physical form through your crown. . . . Be sure to ground and center before opening your eyes.*]

CAT

Love of Self

Cats are independent and cannot be controlled, which gives them an air of mystery that lends credence to their reputation as good familiars for witches. Familiars are creatures, usually animals, that serve as both helper and companion to someone in the work of magic. Unlike some other animals, cats are not afraid of unseen spirit beings, and they have excellent telepathic communications with humans. House cats are often drawn to spiritual energy, especially when that energy is being used for healing or in ceremony. Their purr is a healing vibration that is especially effective when they lie on the part of you that is hurting. The underlying bond that connects a cat to a witch, or to a healing need, is love, and Cat's journey in the Cauldron is about self-love.

Cats are extremely psychic, and in nineteenth-century England, people made sure their children played with cats to help develop their clairvoyant capabilities. There has long been a belief that cats have strong mediumistic powers, an attribute that has been associated with the beauty of their eyes. Yet it can also be suggested that their domestication has allowed them the luxury of time to develop their natural psychic powers.

Cats were first domesticated by the Egyptians and were immediately accepted into the temples and households, where they were pampered and spoiled. They, in return, guarded the granaries from rodents and kept the households free of snakes. Cats came to be considered so sacred that when they died, they were mummified and buried in special cat cemeteries with elaborate funerary rites.

The cat goddess of the Egyptian pantheon is Bast, a goddess of fertility and sexuality, as well as of motherhood and love. She is also known for her abilities as a healer. Bastet is a facet, or manifestation, of Bast, and it is she who guides us through this Cauldron journey. When she brought this journey into the Cauldron, Bastet appeared as a large, slender, dark gray cat with very pointed ears. She wore a jeweled collar and seemed very pleased with herself. Her journey is about self-love and helps you learn to love yourself as she loves herself. She says that until you can love yourself, you can love no one. You may be dependent, in lust, attached, or even dominating, but you cannot, on an equal-to-equal basis, love another until you learn self-love.

Bastet will take you to a place of magic mirrors and show you particular aspects of yourself. After you have taken this journey and as you become more comfortable with it, you can explore other images in your mirrors. Try your wise old self, your child self, your sexual self, and others as relevant. Ask Thoth to help you interpret the reflections.

Cat Journey

[*Proceed with the alchemy. . . .*]

Thoth is there, petting Bastet, the cat that is lying entwined around his feet. Thoth gives her back one last rub and smiles at you.

Follow Bastet as she leads you along a path heading upstream beside a swiftly moving creek. This path is well worn, though narrow, and you know that she follows it often to the place where she is taking you. You come to the base of a waterfall, and off to one side there is a pool of still, dark water. Bastet looks in and touches her image with one paw. As you sit on the edge of the bank and look into the water, see your reflection clearly—the way you would like to see yourself. The image is wavery and does not hold still. Slowly it fades into the image of yourself as you really are. . . .

As you continue to gaze into the pond, the still waters begin to spiral, pulling your image down, pulling your vision down to below the waters. . . .

With a splash, Bastet jumps into the water, down into the center of the spiraling vortex. . . . Follow her, and to your surprise, you will realize that the water is no more. You will see that it is only illusion, and you fall gently to the ground of the cavern under the illusion. . . .

Bastet waits in an entrance to a tunnel, her head turned toward you, her body ready to go forward. Scramble up and follow her, continuing down the tunnel, which gets darker and darker. As the darkness becomes complete, you come up against a hard, smooth surface.

It begins to get lighter, and you see that you are in a hall of mirrors. As Bastet prances from one mirror to another, you realize that these are no ordinary mirrors. They reflect much deeper than the outside of your body.

There are seven mirrors. Each one mirrors a different image. Take the time you need to look at yourself in each of the seven mirrors, inspecting each view:

> The first shows you how you think you look. . . .
> The second shows you how you really look. . . .
> The third shows you the soul view of yourself. . . .
> The fourth shows the heart view. . . .
> The fifth shows your chakra system in full color. . . .
> The sixth shows you your true self, the best potential self
>   you could be. . . .
> The seventh is your unified self, at one with the universe. . . .

Follow Bastet as she steps into and walks through the last mirror, into a clearing where your friends and family wait. Go to each one and touch them. See yourself as they see you. Experience each view in its fullness. . . . [*Long pause.*]

The Great Mother enters the grove and holds out her hands to you. As you touch her, experience the love she has for herself, which is the same love she has for you. Realize that by loving yourself, you can love all of creation, as a part of you, and can be loved in return, as part of the creation of all.

Bastet wraps herself around your legs. Reach down to pet her soft fur. You may wish to give her a gift. . . .

She leads you back to Thoth. Take a moment with Thoth to gain deeper understanding of the images. . . .

[*Thoth will help you return to your body when you are ready. . . .*]

WERNEKE © 1991

SALMON

Energy/Fertility

Grandfather Salmon is very old. He has been around since there was more sea than land, and he has adapted to a wide range of environments around the world. Wherever he thrives, Salmon is a symbol of renewal, returning year after year to remind people of the ongoing cycles of giving and receiving in life. Regardless of the difficulties, nothing deflects him from his commitment.

Native Americans of the Pacific Northwest consider salmon sacred. These tribes are richly diversified and cultured, in part due to the former abundance of salmon. They could depend on them to return each year and provide sustenance. Because they could preserve their catch and meet their yearly food needs in a few months, they had time to develop other interests, including art and ceremonies.

Life for many of these tribes revolved around salmon, especially during spawning season. They believed that salmon were a race of immortals who turned themselves into fish each spring to swim upstream to feed the people. The bones that remained after the feasting were offered back to the river, so that the spirit of Salmon could be carried back out to sea, enabling the process to be repeated at the same time the following year.

Salmon are extremely adaptable, adjusting as they move from saltwater to sweet water as they fight their way upstream to spawn. Because of the proliferation of dams, the harvesting of the forests, and the dramatic influx of people along the rivers where they spawn, many species of salmon have been severely reduced in numbers, and some are facing extinction.

Salmon brings many gifts into the Cauldron. This journey conveys empowerment, energy, and fertility. Salmon has strength, a sense of purpose, and the intuitive abilities to know exactly where he needs to go and how to get there. He always returns to the place of his birth to spawn. Try this spawning journey for fertile dreams, goal setting, self-actualization, and fertility affirmations.

Salmon Journey

[*Do the alchemy*. . . .]

Thoth sends you through an opening in space, and you drop right into icy cold water. As your head gets wet, the cold rushes down your body to what would be your feet, and you realize that instead of feet you have a tail. You are a salmon swimming under the water, parallel with the ripples on the water, just a couple of inches beneath the surface. Take some time to acclimate to being a salmon, getting the feel of your body and its relationship to the swiftly moving water of the river. You are swimming upstream, against the current. . . .

Notice the way energy moves in your salmon body. You can feel it moving from head to tail down your back and down your stomach. The ridge on your back senses the warmth at the upper part of the water, while the one on your stomach picks up the coolness of the deeper water. The two ridges, completely separate, register the different temperatures above and below simultaneously. This sensitivity at the two ridges creates a boundary that distinguishes finite stimulation both from above and from below.

Sensory stimulation is being read along those ridges while the movement of your body retains flexibility from side to side. The awareness of that duality—of both of these things going on at once—blows apart the stiff and stale energy flowing throughout your body. As you're reading up and down, you are weaving from side to side in the motion of swimming, creating the explosive emission of stuck energy. . . .

As you move into the balance of those two flows, you are able to see and feel your relationship between the movements within your body, in three dimensions. It registers to your senses as though energy is moving constantly through your chakra system, turning on all your channels and connecting your consciousness with your DNA. . . . The experience of the synergistic polarity is so intense that you feel as though you can pass it on to your children. At the point when you feel it at peak strength, the energy starts to build in your tail and genitals. Sparks of fire run up your center, stimulating a fierce desire to succeed. The energy seems to dance up your DNA spiral as though it were a rainbow. You can feel it dancing its way up through your spine and out your crown. . . . It is possible to experience orgasm or tantric release as the energy spews out your crown and flows down your outer self as opalescent, rainbow energy. . . . This luminescence is reflected in your skin, your pearlescent outer glow.

The energy carries you back on the return trip, feeling relaxed and light. . . . Flow back to where Thoth waits for you. Spend a moment discussing this experience with him. . . .

[*Thoth will assist you back into your physical form. . . .*]

PART IV

JOURNEYS FOR
TRANSFORMATION

In this section of Power Animal Meditations, *you can work on situations and problems in your life that require change, learning how to turn adversity into advantage, and how to use the alchemy to create what you want and need in your life.*

BUTTERFLY
Transformation/Self-Esteem

Butterfly represents metamorphosis, going within to come out whole again. Ancient symbols for the soul, butterflies were thought to be inhabited by the souls of humans while they searched for new incarnations; in classical Greek, the word for "butterfly" and "soul" is the same. The butterfly also represents freedom: After entering into the dark void of the cocoon, it emerges bright and free, living the great mystery of its metamorphosis. All the stages of its development are displayed prominently on its fluttering message.

The stages of the butterfly's metamorphosis correspond to the stages of human spiritual growth. As the larvae, we are still unconscious of all but what is right in front of us. We go into the inner depths of ourselves in the cocoon to pupate, and when we break that shell and take flight, we are freed spiritually to share our joy with all the world.

Butterflies are also a symbol of fragility, more for their transparency to light than for any intrinsic weakness. They are, however, an indicator species, not strong enough to escape the ravages upon their environments. Because of deforestation and pesticides, many varieties of butterflies are becoming extinct. One such species, the Queen Alexandra's Bird-Winged Butterfly, was discovered in Papua, New Guinea, by a Danish explorer as recently as the 1940s. We have barely discovered its existence and know very little about it, yet it is already endangered by encroaching civilization. This bird-winged butterfly has a wingspread of one-and-a-half to two feet and is nocturnal in its habits. The males are brilliantly colored with red, turquoise, and gold markings. The Gimi tribe, the butterfly's only human neighbors, is also nearing extinction. Both live in a palm forest near the shore. The palm trees, the primary source of food and shelter for these butterflies, are being decimated for palm oil.

Butterflies stand for freedom and spirit, yet they have been long sought after as specimens for their beauty. The bird-winged butterflies are especially desirable because of their immense size. There are now breeding programs designed ostensibly to preserve the species while keeping them enslaved, feeding the materialism of those who would take their souls while piercing their hearts for their display cases.

The Rainbow Butterfly that brought this journey to the Cauldron helps build self-esteem. People who are afraid to see the real face within their own being spend tremendous energy creating and keeping up masks to hide behind. The transformative qualities of the Rainbow Butterfly make it a great ally for building the kind of self-esteem that allows people to be themselves and to appreciate their own beauty.

Take an idea or concept of what you want to be and how you want to see yourself, then take this journey and go within. When you break out of your cocoon, you will have become that which you intended. The costume that the butterfly brings back from within the darkness and mystery of the cocoon is the beauty of the spirit of yourself in all your glory. The metamorphosis of Butterfly is about the mystery of what happens when you go within to the darkness to manifest the beauty you were born to create.

Butterfly Journey

Use the regular Cauldron alchemy, but this time when the steam condenses through the crown, it will be into a very fine beam of light. . . . As you come up this beam through your crown, you enter a cocoon, guided and protected by Thoth. . . . Within this cocoon you are gently and softly held in place as though wrapped in soft, crystalline gauze. An ever-present heartbeat marks time as you pupate in your silken womb. . . . [*Pause.*]

Approaching the final stage of metamorphosis, you can see reflections or flickering colored lights, which are the radiance of your self against the crystalline fibers of the cocoon, providing an opportunity to glimpse your inner beauty. There is a passing of energy as this radiance hits the fibers of the cocoon. It bounces back and mirrors the divine creation that you are, literally recoding through self-esteem. Enjoy and bask in this radiance and brightness of colors that penetrates the darkness of your cocoon. . . . [*Long pause.*]

The walls of the cocoon start to disintegrate. As they fall away, you begin to stretch your wings. This is a slow process, for you are wet and need time to dry. Open your arms wide and experience your colorful wings as they unfurl. They are exquisite. Feel the energy in them and delight in their colorful patterns. Enjoy the exhilaration as your bonds are lifted and you release yourself to flight. . . . You are a magnificent butterfly. This form stays with you always. Take some time now to experience your flight while you dance in the sunlight like a flying flower. . . . [*Long pause.*]

When you are ready, wrap your butterfly wings around your body and slide back into your human form, taking the radiance of your beautiful butterfly with you.

Take a moment with Thoth to share your experience. . . .

[*Thoth will assist you back into ordinary consciousness. . . .*]

Owl
Alchemy/Night Vision

Owls are one of the most controversial birds, evoking a gamut of associations ranging from death, fear, and ill omens to wisdom, protection, and victory. The "wise old owl" is connected with the Greek goddess Athena and is often seen sitting on her shoulder as the embodiment of the cool, clear, and balanced intellect of the North Wind. Many indigenous traditions fear Owl as a harbinger of death, yet she teaches us about change and transformation and can help us overcome our fear of the transformation that we call death.

Owl is a silent-winged huntress of the night who swoops through the thickest forest on velvet wings. Although best known for her keen night vision, she can see equally well in the light.

In the Golden Cauldron, Owl is the doorway into the unknown. Night is a time of rest for most creatures, but in the presence of the moon, when the trees are sleeping and everything is in repose, you can change things. You can recast the pieces of your life. In this journey, Owl takes you to a place of alchemy, where you can turn lead into gold, metaphorically speaking. The true alchemy is about taking the raw, base material of which we are made and transforming ourselves into the alchemical gold—the philosopher's stone, enlightenment. From Owl, you become aware of all aspects of the power of change, so that you can observe and feel where shifts occur. In some ways, the *process* of change is more important than the outcome.

It is important to consider very carefully what aspect of yourself you choose to work on during your journey with Owl, for if her power is used in a harmful way, it will most definitely return to hurt the perpetrator. It is important to stay only long enough to get the answer for the change that you request. Ask only one question per journey, and choose the issue you want to work on before you travel to meet Owl. This journey is somewhat complex and requires both experience and clarity of intent. Keep your mind empty, clear, and free in order to let something new enter, and you will learn something about the quality of receptivity.

Owl can also see the ley lines in the earth. She lives between the worlds and can bring light into dark places. She teaches you to create space in the things that are too dense to allow light in. When you let light in, you can see in the dark. It is useful to work with Owl to regenerate sight, both physical and psychic. Although this journey is concerned with *sight*, when you return another time she may do the same process with *hearing*, for owls have clairaudient abilities as well.

Owl Journey

[*Do the Cauldron alchemy.* . . .]

Thoth is wearing feathers and dancing. Owl appears—first her face, then her body, and now you can see the entire owl. She's white with dappled wings, which are brownish at the tips. Her eyes are dark and stare at you unblinking. It's as though you are looking into space rather than eyes, and you are drawn into the passageway of her wide pupils. When you maintain eye contact, Owl changes from animal to symbol, taking on a larger-than-life, magnificent presence. Her wings are spread outward. She is the doorway into the dark world on the other side. As you pass through the deep beams of her eyes, you can see stars. The darkness is not black but, rather, a thick, night blue.

Ahead looms a giant, clear pyramid with prismatic qualities. As you approach it, you are aware that light, coming from a large star some distance away, passes into it. Watch the light closely, for it is refracted from the pyramid at an angle, and it has rainbows in it. Pay attention to how the light enters the pyramid. Rainbow fragments of the white light you are watching are going on a trajectory toward the pyramid and enter easily. Once the light enters, it is transformed; you can observe the change in its quality. . . .

Feel yourself drawn toward the pyramid. To enter, you must slow down the light by slowing down time. You are on the level of the particles of light, and as you see them going into the crystal pyramid, you can easily follow. . . .

Inside the pyramid you have become Owl. Feel the feathers on your head. Your arms are outstretched wings, silent and strong. The pyramid is a place for alchemy, a place where you can take things you don't like about yourself and turn them into assets. Take a moment now to work on the one issue you brought with you into this journey. . . . [*Long pause.*]

When this part of the journey is complete, fly up to the point at the top of the pyramid. Your owl self shoots out the tip into the night sky, circling in great spirals until you enter a forest. . . . As you fly into these woods, the light of the moon and stars disappears. On silent wings, you swoop between the trees. You can see as clearly as if your eyes shone infrared rays, penetrating all matter to touch the life force within.

Land on the branch of a large tree that feels like home. From your perch, look out upon the forest and see that all is well. Everywhere you look, the forest is peaceful. You can distinguish the rocks from the other living matter by their density. Take a few minutes to play with this new ability to see the life within the darkness and underneath the covering of matter. . . . [*Long pause.*]

When it is time to return, you hear Thoth hoot like an owl. Respond and fly back to where he waits. . . . Transform back into your human form and spend a few moments with him, discussing your experience and receiving further guidance he might have for you at this time. . . .

[*Thoth will assist you back into your body. . . .*]

WERNEKE © 1991

PERSIAN LEOPARD
Grief

The Persian leopard is a subspecies of leopard that used to range throughout central and northern Iran. The variety found in the mountains of northern Iran is larger, with magnificent long fur, whereas in central Iran the leopard is small, light colored, and shorthaired. These leopards' coats have always been highly prized, and warriors used to wear their pelts in battle. Today's fashion demands have promoted relentless hunts that, although illegal, have brought about the impending extinction of these graceful creatures.

Grief is a great teacher and an unavoidable part of our lives. Persian Leopard understands grief from her experience of becoming nearly extinct. Although some Persian leopards are being bred successfully in captivity, there are very few left in the wild. She is, therefore, an ideal ally through which you can access and deal with unresolved sorrow and other grief issues.

Fear of grief and extinction often keep people in line and stuck. Both are potent forces with powerful impact. Each person who suffers loss is ultimately alone in his or her grief. Our culture neither honors nor defines the process for us. Many people respond to their sorrow by looking to others to show them how they are supposed to feel, rather than honoring the feelings that naturally occur.

Grief binds you to the person you are grieving about. In the following journey, you have an opportunity to unbind yourself without diminishing the relationship. Sometimes you have direct contact with the person for whom you are grieving.

When you go through the door and reexperience the causes of grief, you can change what you can't handle, for this everyday reality is only one level of existence. It can be modified in the many alternate levels of reality. The leopard that is becoming extinct here is not extinct in other places, other realities, where different choices were made.

It is important that you ground yourself thoroughly and protect the space in which you are working when you take this journey. You can do this by calling on all the animals from the Cauldron to shield and guard your space during this process. It is also helpful to smudge the space with cedar, sage, sweetgrass, or other appropriate incense.

Persian Leopard Journey

[*Do the alchemy. . . .*]

When you come out of the alchemy, the Crone is there. You can see only her left hand, which bears a green- or red-stoned ring. She has her hand on Persian Leopard, caged and alone. You have an immediate sense of grief in the presence of this large, graceful, trapped cat, surrounded by the bars of the cage. There is loneliness and a feeling of grief in her solitude, in her awareness of the dwindling numbers of her kind. You can sense the loss by the heaviness in your heart and chest. Your emotions are stirred. . . .

Persian Leopard invites you to come into the cage where she is and feel how it is to be alone and virtually extinct. In this close proximity, you are able to share her grief, her knowledge that all her children have been hunted. She is torn apart inside. Feel her grief in your body. There is a sense of shock and disbelief as you realize the pain of her suffering and become aware of your own mortality and fear of obliteration or loss. . . . [*Pause.*]

Loneliness weighs upon you with the weight of her species. Look about for a way out, a way to release this heavy burden of grief. . . . When you come out the other side of the incredible emotion of loneliness, there is a release, a letting go. . . . [*Pause.*]

The Crone comes fully into form now and takes you into your heart center, where the eternal flame of life burns upon the altar of your most sacred temple. You have an opportunity now, with the support of the Crone and Persian Leopard, to take your negative feelings of grief and place them on the flame. You must decide which parts of your own grief and sadness you are willing to release at this time. You can focus on particular griefs, negativity, loneliness, or whatever comes up as appropriate. This part of the process can be very potent, and you may feel physical changes in your body while this is happening. . . . [*Pause.*]

Sometimes your deepest griefs are hidden behind closed doors. If you choose, those doors can be safely opened at this time so that you can deal with issues that are otherwise difficult to access. As you put your grief upon the flame, you may have to reexperience some of the more difficult situations that caused these feelings, yet you are comforted by the presence of Persian Leopard and the Crone. During the re-creation of your experience, you may have direct interaction with those for whom you are grieving. Listen to the message they give you at this time. . . . [*Long pause.*]

Persian Leopard has a further message for you, for she has insight into your situation. . . . [*Pause.*]

You may give her a suitable gift, possibly one that can bring new growth and energy to her species. . . .

The Crone places her hand on your head and gives you a blessing. . . .

Thoth appears and spends a moment with you as you recount your experience.

[*Thoth assists you back into your body.* . . .]

WERNEKE © 1991

Snow Leopard
Fear

Snow Leopard is a magnificent, mysterious huntress of the Himalayas, elusive and rare. The following quote is from Snow Leopard, exactly as she introduced herself to me.

My name is Scimitar. I am a snow leopard. I am here to bring fear into your life. Like the icy north wind I live. When you hear me scream, you will know I am stalking you. The blood in your veins will turn into ice. I will pursue you relentlessly. I will stalk you without ceasing, no matter where you go or which way you turn. I will be there gazing into your eyes. Feel the fear. Do you feel the sense of panic? If you don't, you should, because I am here to devour your guts. I am a hunting feline. When I capture my prey, I disembowel its soft belly with my hind claws. I will shred you; I will force you to deal with your innermost fears. I will find you wherever you run—in the cities or in the mountains. I will make you wait. I will take my time and tease you.

Only when you have finally stopped running, when you have looked at your fear and found that place in you that knows you have no alternative but to stand fully firm and face me, will I slowly walk up to you, gaze into your eyes with my green eyes, and knock you down.

Through your fear of me, I will take you places and you will learn things about yourself that nothing else can teach you but fear. Once you have faced me, I will curl up by your side to keep you warm and walk with you wherever you go, being your companion warrior when a warrior is needed.

Do not embark upon this journey lightly. Put yourself in a place of total safety without distraction. The journey may take a long time.

This work, just like life, cannot be all comfort and ease. Sometimes it takes fear—being backed up against the wall—for you to look for and discover resources that were previously unknown to you. Fear also exposes the parts of yourself you try to keep hidden. If you have the courage to take the following journey with Snow Leopard and later on are cornered, and if you have the courage to look her in the eye, you will discover that her eyes are mirrors reflecting the parts of you that need growth, the parts you that try to run and hide from, the uncomfortable parts.

She may reach out and rip a piece of you loose and show it to you as she plays with it, just as a cat does with a mouse. Do not take this journey if you are not willing to see the sides of yourself that make you uncomfortable, but also know that without acknowledging and bringing these areas into light, you can grow only so far.

Snow leopards often disembowel their prey. What do the intestines symbolize for us? Usually the symbolism has to do with sickness or toxins, the parts of ourselves that are being eliminated, or our waste products. It also relates to gut fear. During this journey notice those places in your body where you experience fear, and pay attention to your instinctual behavior. You may be surprised to find it to be different from what you expected.

Once you've worked out your fears with Snow Leopard, you gain the perception of a cat—the clarity and sharpness of felines. The realm of cats opens one's awareness and sensitivity. There is a combined strength and gentleness, and a knowing of when to use each. In the Cauldron, Snow Leopard is the doorway. Each person passes her inspection before being permitted into the realm of cats. Every experience of her will be different, depending on what she sees as fitting for the moment.

Snow Leopard is a loner and comes in a totally silent approach. Living high in the Himalayas, snow leopards are extremely rare, avoiding all contact with humans. It is a great quest to find one, and the value of their hides has made poaching extremely lucrative, although it is illegal. This wanton hunting has been devastating to this species, which is, as a result, endangered.

Fear is a great, although often misunderstood, teacher. Being afraid is not the same as being a coward. It takes courage, however, to face your fears and let them move through you. In Snow Leopard's journey, you are asked to look at fear, to feel it and know it, and then to make peace with it, for there is no escape. Fear is a lonely experience in that you must deal with it yourself.

If you can, do this journey alone in the woods at night. If not, you can create that place anywhere, even in your imagination.

Snow Leopard Journey

[*Find the appropriate power place that you want to be in to do this work. . . . When you come out of the Cauldron alchemy, it is twilight. . . .*] As your sight comes into focus, you see that you are on a mountain path in a very rocky area with lots of maze-like trails. Darkness is encroaching as you look for a safe place to make camp for the night.

In the stillness of the in-between time, you begin to think of the things you are afraid of. . . . [*Pause.*] You sense the presence of something or someone nearby, watching you. . . . A stone falls, and you feel as though you are being stalked. . . .

Suddenly, from above and to your right, a scream rends the evening stillness and fills you with terror. There is only one who screams like that: Snow Leopard. . . . You start running on the trail to your left, thinking maybe you've gotten away. When you see a blur of movement to your right, you realize she has leapt to the rock directly in front of you. You stand frozen, the two of you locked in a gaze, her emerald eyes gleaming. . . .

She is hunting. . . . She is hunting you. . . . Turn around and run. There is a narrow passage in the rocks to your right. You squeeze through, hoping it's too narrow for her to come after you. Stand still. Each breath feels like a betrayal. As you attempt to quiet your breath, rocks fall from above, and you know she is coming. You turn to run back the way you came, and she swipes down with her forepaw and rips your scalp. Blood pours down your face. Taste the salty ironness of your own blood. You become frantic, and your terror increases as you realize she is playing with you. Follow yet another trail. It takes a sharp corner and ends in a solid wall of rock. You are trapped. . . .

As you turn around with your back to the rock wall, you see her coming for you. There is no terror in her eyes. She comes closer and closer, her tail switching back and forth. You scramble, your fingernails ripping at the rock wall, trying to find anything to make a weapon to defend yourself. At the same time, you know you are hers. You are locked into her eyes as she stares at you, her gaze penetrating your very being. This seems to last an eternity. . . .

At last she pounces, and with one swipe of her front paw she has ripped open your abdomen and your intestines are spilling out. . . .

In this eternal moment beyond panic, you will be forced to see yourself as you are. . . . She puts one big paw on your chest and stares at you. Any time you attempt to move, her claws extend to stop you. . . .

When you finally accede to the moment and realize that this is it— there is no way out, you are going to die—you can meet her gaze with total acceptance. Consciously open your heart and relax your entire physical body. Pull your head back and bare your throat to her. . . . Snow Leopard retracts her claws a little bit, calmly starts licking the blood oozing from your body, and then looks up at you, her gold-green eyes glowing through the darkness.

Be with Snow Leopard and receive a further teaching about your relationship with fear. . . . [*Long pause.*]

She nuzzles you and purrs as you realize this bonding process is complete. A sense of exhilaration pervades your spirit as you recognize the breakthrough you have made. . . .

When you have completed your experience with Snow Leopard, Thoth will be there. Take a moment to discuss this experience with him. . . .

[*Thoth will assist you back into your body. . . . You feel safe and secure, as though you could accomplish anything. . . . Ground and center. . . .*]

CROCODILE

Getting What You Want

In Egypt, the crocodile was revered as the god Sobek. He is a very important, although often misunderstood, character in the Egyptian pantheon.

When you need to regain your balance, Sobek is an appropriate ally. His work relates to the brain. In humans, the hypothalamus corresponds to the reptilian brain. Sobek's strong healing potential is associated with the hypothalamus, the part of the brain that controls the autonomic nervous system—the glands, smooth muscles, and all the unconscious functions. Sobek is king here; he's in control of these functions. This places him in a key position to communicate with the body. The conscious mind has the ability to communicate with the unconscious mind. We usually perceive this as gut feelings, or intuition.

Sobek, from his seat of power at the hypothalamus, is the intermediary between the nervous and endocrine systems, glands, and hormones. He detects changes in the body and directs the hormones. The hypothalamus is at the center of the mind-over-body phenomenon. The reptilian brain is about primal emotions—rage, aggression, sex, and all drives related to our more animal side. It also controls body temperature.

Because the hypothalamus regulates biological rhythms, Sobek is closely connected to the natural ebb and flow of things. His part of the brain is known as the "feeding center," which tells you whether or not you are hungry, enabling Sobek to help you with certain digestive problems. Thirst centers and waking/sleep functions are included in his sphere of influence as well.

To become divine, we have to accept our animal self and balance our reptile self. The crocodile is the highest development of the reptile, the overseer of the reptilian part of our brain. He provides the connection that links the intuitive with the scientific modes.

Your fear of crocodiles can be diminished by recognition of your self-determination and Sobek's sense of humor, which is more reptilian than cerebral and is based on pleasure. His jokes are usually related to his own being and are often childlike.

The journey that Sobek has brought into the Cauldron has to do with getting what you want. It is very powerful and should not be overused. Once you learn how Crocodile achieves his goals, be selective about how often you use the technique, and have your goal in mind when you undertake to visit Sobek. Ask for only one thing each time you take this journey, so that you can focus precisely on what you want. And remember, be careful what you ask for, because you just might get it!

Sobek's Journey

[*Do the alchemy. . . .*]

When you come out of the alchemy, Thoth takes you to a temple in Egypt, along the Nile. Along the side of the temple there are steps leading down to the edge of a very big natural pond or lake with reeds and other water foliage.

Many pairs of eyes look at you from out of the water. Now you can see some of the faces, the tops of the heads of crocodiles. They begin swimming around, creating a funnel, a vortex in the water. They beckon you with their tails, indicating for you to jump into the middle of the whirlpool that they create. . . . Jump.

You're being pulled down, down, down—still further down. It's no longer water but crocodile skin that surrounds you. The sides of the whorl are surfaced with crocodiles. As you swirl, you turn into a crocodile. The feeling is reptilian, different from a mammal, yet also different from a snake. Become aware of the scales on your long body and the huge claws on your feet. You can't see ahead very well, but you can see to the sides and roll your eyes on the sides of your head. Stretch your jaws out really wide. Let yourself become comfortable with your teeth and your large size and shape. . . .

Sit with your jaws half open, your eyes half rolled. Relax and check things out from your crocodilian point of view. The whirlpool has stopped. Other crocodiles are around, lurking in the water. Notice how they communicate with one another. . . .

From Crocodile, you can learn to be observant, to see more clearly, to pounce when the time is right, and to be patient until that time. While you're being patient, think about just what it is that you want. Begin to store up energy, biding time while you prepare to strike. Notice how you store energy and build tension within the languor. Outside you are relaxed, waiting patiently, yet your calm exterior is like a shell around a bomb.

Stay attentive to the building of tension within Crocodile's waiting game. You know what it is you are after. Feel the building of this force, the gathering of the power. It starts in the middle of your stomach and spreads out, like blowing up a balloon. When it's ready, you feel full. Your body is brimming, puffed up, even to your eyes. You quiver with the fullness of the power that has gathered inside you.

Bring into focus exactly what you want. You have already identified it while in your laid-back, relaxed state. You have the ability to know exactly when to move, when it's time to unleash that stored energy. Now bring what you want clearly into focus—and go for it! You spring like a steel trap instantly released to its objective. . . . [*Long pause.*]

When you have completed your work as Crocodile, lash your tail a couple of times to connect with the whirlpool. You are pulled, sucked back into the whirlpool—back, back, back, up to the edge of the pond. You will find your self on the bank as Crocodile flips himself into the pond.

Give an offering of food to your crocodile friend. . . . Receive any further message he might have for you at this time.

Thoth is there to discuss this experience with you. . . .

[*When it is time, Thoth will help you back into your body. . . .*]

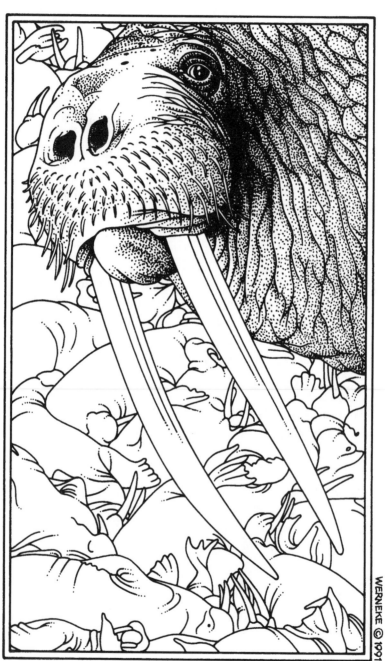

WERNEKE © 1991

WALRUS
Relationship with Money

Walrus has come to help heal our relationships with money. For this journey, he showed up looking a little like a banker, sporting whiskers but no cigar. His domain is abundant sea. Walrus symbolizes money because of the bounty of his body, which offers abundance to those who hunt him. His tusks, usually used for uprooting mollusks and clams from the ocean floor, are sought after for ivory. His blubber produces oil to create warmth and light.

While they may appear to us as somewhat cantankerous, one can understand that walruses, although normally placid, might attack humans when they feel threatened. For Eskimos living along the Arctic coast from Alaska to Greenland, walrus hunting was dangerous, but well worth the risk. From their bones were crafted the harpoon hooks that were used to kill them. Their meat was stored and fed to the sled dogs, and their hides were used to cover the hulls of the Eskimos' boats. From their teeth and tusks were fashioned fishhooks, combs, and other tools, and their ivory was especially favored for the scrimshaw carvings of Eskimo craftsmen.

Walrus is comfortable with the idea of money and views it as one more tool to be brought into balance, both personally and on a planetary level. When you resist money you block the flow of energy, causing barriers and sickness to occur. Attempting to own or control money in a frugal way changes the free flow of energy, creating imbalances. Greed leads to killing many species for the money their body parts bring. Although saving money brings security, it must be done consciously and with good intentions, or, once again, imbalances develop.

As you heal your relationship with money, your energy level will increase. Walrus can help you with your investments by showing you how to manage your monetary assets properly. He can assist you in negotiating business deals and is very helpful for people managing their own businesses.

Walruses are herding animals that migrate annually. Although we perceive them as clumsy on land, they swim quite gracefully. They can travel vast distances in the sea because they know where the currents are and how to get into the natural flow and movements in water. Often, instead of swimming, they prefer to hitch rides on ice floes as they move northward. Walrus can teach you how to follow the path of least resistance to open things up and get energy moving. Walrus medicine has to do with energy and how it flows. As a healer, he is especially helpful for those with high blood pressure and hypertension, for he can show how to unclog arteries and get the currents in the body flowing.

Before taking this journey, take a few moments to bring into focus your issues around money and what it means to you.

Walrus Journey

[*Do the alchemy. . . .*]

Ask Thoth to direct you to Walrus, and he will point to the icy shores along an arctic beach. The landscape is flat and white, with the exception of large, tall boulders rounded by the incessant flow of water, ice, and snow. The shoreline imperceptibly joins the equally pale sky. The weak arctic sun warms the walruses as they lie on the stark beach, close to the pounding waves and rocks.

The first thing you notice when you see the walruses is their massive size. Your attention is drawn to a particular walrus. It may be one of the big bulls lying opulently in the sun or perhaps a smaller cow. As you look into the eyes of this new walrus friend, you connect and experience a type of bonding. Your senses become more acute, and you begin to hear the sounds of walruses more clearly, discovering that you have an inherent knowledge of their language. Your walrus friend invites you closer and you see his great tusks, his whiskers, and the folds of his blubbery skin. Walrus offers his friendship. . . .

Take a few moments to commune with Walrus, and he will give you insight into how you can deal with money in a more productive and healing way. He will give you information about your current monetary situation and how he can assist you in your dealings with money. . . . [*Long pause.*]

Walrus is likely to expect you to use the information you are given. Be sure to take him with you when dealing with the issues touched upon in this journey. He offers you a small carving of himself as a fetish you can keep with you so that whenever you need advice, you can call upon him. . . .

Walrus may share other healing techniques with you. For example, he might show you how to remove energy blocks or how to use energy once you tap into it. Be willing to be surprised. . . . [*Long pause.*]

To thank Walrus, consider sending energy from your heart out to the planet to help the imbalances caused by the improper use of money. When you are ready, ask for Thoth. Discuss your experience with him. . . .

[*Thoth will help you return to your body. . . .*]

WERNEKE © 1991

KANGAROO
Balancing Evil

One of the first Australian animals one thinks of is the kangaroo, a common marsupial that roams about the countryside in much the same way as do deer in North America; there are more than sixty species of them. Kangaroos are to the aborigines what buffalo were to Native Americans: both symbolize abundance. Like the buffalo once did, these wonderful animals provide food, fiber, clothing, and tools. Many of the dances and ceremonies of the aborigines depict kangaroo hunts or behavior. Unfortunately, kangaroos are regarded as pests by many people, who simply shoot them for sport to get rid of them.

Kangaroos are very powerful allies. When you are aware of some evil on the planet, you can take your grievance to the kangaroos, and they will set up an ancient ritual as a way of counterbalancing evil that humans have perpetrated. Be selective about what issues you choose to bring before them.

This is a journey of exploration into the aboriginal "Upperworld." Every time you return to the kangaroos, you will gain a deeper understanding of the nature of these wonderful creatures and the connection they have given you to the Upperworld.

Playing a tape of didgeridoo music in the background can enhance this journey.

Kangaroo Journey

[*Do the alchemy. . . .*]
Thoth is wearing kangaroo skins on his feet and shoulders. You look out across a vast range containing many kangaroos. Accustom yourself

to the wide open rangeland. In the distance, you see devil winds—dark, whirling funnels announcing the arrival of a storm. This activity signals the kangaroos, who seem to come from all directions to a place quite near you where there is an opening into the earth. As you get closer, you realize that many of these are people wearing kangaroo skins. Go with the kangaroos as they enter an ancient, secret meeting place deep in a cavern beneath the surface of the earth. You are "down under," literally, and there is some kind of clan ceremony in progress. You can hear the low, vibrating drone of a didgeridoo.

All of the kangaroos create a circle, and you become part of that circle. In the center is a ground painting, black and red and white, forming an abstract design in a circular shape. The image of this ground painting may shift as the ceremony continues. Open your heart and express what it is that troubles you—what evil you have seen that requires the attention of these powerful allies. . . . [Pause.]

You are given a teaching about the particular situation you have brought to this council. . . . Take heed—you may also be given instructions as to something that you can do to help. . . .

Out from the shadows, a medicine spirit wearing a mask enters the center of the circle. This spirit is a small person with a very large head. He has wild hair, white and fuzzy and matted. His body appears gray, as though powdered with a chalky substance. He is a very fierce warrior.

He begins to move around the center of the circle, presenting colored strings to all who sit with him. These strings generate from his belly, like umbilical cords. Hold your string tightly and carefully in your hand. When everyone has their strings, the medicine spirit steps upon his right foot and begins to move in an upward and outward spiral. Everyone follows, feeling themselves lifted off the ground. The spiral begins to gain speed and height. As you feel yourself spiraling, revolving up through the crust of the earth above the plains, above the storm, your circle spreads out, the umbilical cords appearing to stretch as you gain height with each revolution.

As you go still higher above the earth's surface, you can see the continent of Australia beneath you. Your perspective changes as you reach a height from which the entire globe is visible. From here, looking upward, you can see the stars clearly in the darkness of space. It is as though you have journeyed to the crack in the world, the space between, from where you can communicate directly with the Upperworld. The medicine spirit will hold this space for you just long enough for you to receive information or an experience pertinent to your initial request. . . . [*Long pause.*]

When it is time, the spirit changes direction by stepping down on his left foot. Immediately, the entire circle begins to spiral back downward through the clouds and through the crust of the earth to the cavern beneath the surface. . . .

When you have returned, sit once again on the floor of this cave. The threads return back to the medicine spirit.

As you leave the cavern, place your hand, face down, in a depression in the ground by the door that is filled with a thick, red liquid and make your print on the wall. As you do this, become aware of the many handprints covering the walls, the prints of others who have been initiated in this way.

Once back on the range, there are flashes of lightning, and thunder rumbles in the distance.

Thoth meets you on the outback range, and you can discuss this experience with him. . . .

[*Thoth assists you in returning to your ordinary consciousness. . . .*]

WERNEKE © 1991

HONEYBEE
Giving Back to the Earth

Honeybees represent the feminine potency in nature; their honey is the sweetness of love. They are sacred to the Goddess and live in a matriarchy ruled by a queen. Priestesses of Aphrodite were called *melissae,* a word meaning "bees," and priestesses in the Amazon were also sometimes referred to as bees.

The buzzing sound bees make is often associated with the raising of energy leading to the ecstasy of nirvana, and a person lying in a pit covered with bees is a symbol of enlightenment. The bee is a very important sacred symbol in Buddhism, and the Buddha is sometimes depicted as made out of bees.

The many curative attributes of bees contribute to the work of the Goddess, furthering healing and enhancing and protecting our immune systems. The sting of honeybees is said to be a remedy for arthritis, and many other healing possibilities are becoming apparent in light of new research.

Without the honeybee, we wouldn't have flowers and fruits, for bee pollination is a necessary function in the proliferation of nature—what they give is far greater than what they take. Humans can learn not to be greedy from Honeybee.

Bees also give inspiration to people who are studying or working with environmental design, landscape architecture, general architecture, or urban planning in any form. In viewing the natural and appropriate use of space in the hive, we begin to realize how simulated and synthesized human architecture has become, and how much we have altered our planetary environment for what we think of as convenience.

This journey is for people who would like to work with the earth in a more productive and healing way, utilizing natural processes and giving back to the earth. It enables people to buzz on a single idea or aspect of their service while scrutinizing it very carefully and coming to know it better.

Here we strive to understand how we as a community, from small families to a global level, can learn to live in harmony and peace with one another. We explore how we can solve the problems of the world together, not separately. Each time you come you will be given a task that you can take out into the world.

Primarily, however, Honeybee's journey is for all who are interested in actively giving more than they take from Earth.

Bee Journey

[*Do the Cauldron alchemy.* . . .]

Thoth sits in a beautiful garden filled with many different types of flowers. Fruit trees with white and pink blossoms dance in a soft, gentle breeze. It's a warm day, and the sunlight gently blesses the earth. Thoth opens his hand slowly, revealing a honeybee sitting on his palm.

It is fascinating to examine this bee. Study the furry yellow and black bands on its body. Its wings, so seldom still, are now beating in a slow rhythm that captures your consciousness. As you look into its timeless eyes, transform and enter into the body of the bee. . . .

Sharing the body of your new bee friend, you fly toward his hive, which sits in the bowl of a nearby tree. The buzzing sound generated from your wings produces a vibration that is at a communication frequency with the others in the hive. It's an auditory signature that lets them know who you are.

Enter the hive. You are suddenly conscious of the vibrations of a humming resonance. It completely permeates the hive and moves through the surrounding area. . . . Notice how the architecture creates a perfect living environment. This complex natural architecture utilizes concave and convex patterns. The buzzing resounds through the shapes, creating waves that move through your body. . . . [*Pause.*]

Notice also how bees live in harmony with the environment they create and how there is a sense of space in the hive. It does not feel crowded, though there are many bees, all working intently at their parts of the task to maintain the hive. Be aware of the welling of a desire to add your own contribution. . . .

You must now leave the hive to gather pollen. As you make your way to the exit, industrious activity is everywhere. Outside the hive, the garden compels your presence. The sun is an absolute guide for you as you fly from flower to flower, purposefully stopping in the center of each one to gather the pollen. The heady aroma of the flowers mingled with the ecstasy of your flight is utterly delicious. . . .

When you're weighted down with as much pollen as you can carry, return to the hive. As you take the pollen inside, you are stimulated by the tremendous buzz and find yourself dancing your communication about where the good pollen is located to the other bees. . . . [*Pause.*]

You are escorted to the queen's chamber, where you are fed royal jelly and given instructions about your contribution to the community. You will be given a task to complete a full cycle of taking from, and putting back into, the earth. . . .

While in the hive this time, you can begin to view nature from a new perspective, taking on more responsibility and playing a greater role in how you interact with any environment you are in on this planet. As a thank-you to the bees, you can make a decision to do something to help enhance your immediate environment or the earth in some way.

When you next approach the exit of the beehive, ask for Thoth, and you will then find yourself back on the ground in human form by his side. Ask him for any further instructions regarding the teaching you received here. . . .

[*Thoth will assist you back.* . . .]

PART V

HEALING JOURNEYS

These journeys provide an opportunity to explore new ways of healing yourself and others. Many other journeys in Power Animal Meditations *will also contribute to healing, because healing comes naturally as a result of wisdom and knowledge.*

WERNEKE © 1991

BEAR

Dreaming/Crystals/Herbs

Bear is one of the oldest recorded totemic beings, offering nurturing, strength, protection, and wisdom. Many indigenous cultures have myths and customs that show a great respect for Bear. Ancient legends speak of a time when people shared caves with their bear relatives.

Bear is the guardian of the heart chakra of the earth. The journey that she brings to the Cauldron will help increase your awareness of our planet as a living entity. Even those of you who understand the theory of Earth as a living being may not have felt it in your bodies, hearts, and bones. Helping you experience this is Bear's primary function in the following journey.

Once you have felt through every cell of your being the heartbeat of Mother Earth, you will never again be without awareness of the rhythm that connects you to all things. Your emotional body can receive great healing through the recognition of your resonance, your link, with that pulse. Allow it to become a part of your being. Never again must you feel alone or apart from the Mother. Through awareness of this pulse, you can begin to grasp the meaning of time, the inhaling and exhaling of breath like the waves of the ocean, the tides of the earth. It's like putting your head on the breast of one you love. Bear helps you to experience that deep connection.

Some entities can teach you specifically about healing. Thoth is good for that, because understanding and knowledge naturally result in healing. Bear is another. She is an especially helpful ally because she is familiar with the ways of herbs and of crystals that are found deep within the caves where she makes her home.

Bear is a tremendous healing ally. Her deft claws can be used to remove diseased tissue from the body, and she has performed meticulous psychic surgery as part of a spiritual healing team. She often brews potions from her herbal storehouse to alleviate pain or, in some cases, restores memory so that people can find the causes for their illnesses.

Children—and your inner child—will also appreciate playing with Bear. She loves to work with children. I have introduced my bear friend to children as young as four who appreciate bears as both companions and teachers. Sometimes having a bear friend can alleviate fear of the dark and sleeping alone.

My bear friend is called Eawokka. Her name means Bear of the Night Stars. Although she is an old grandmother cinnamon grizzly, each person who journeys to visit Eawokka will envision the kind of bear that is appropriate for them at that time.

To visit Bear through the Cauldron, you must travel into the cold, dark realm of ice and crystals. This journey takes you to a place where you can see and learn about auras similar to the northern lights, the aurora borealis, which is Earth's aura.

With Bear, you can travel to the dark regions where people are most afraid to go. You can learn about and work with crystals here, as there are crystals in her cave that have never been seen or used by humans, as well as clear quartz and other familiar stones.

If you feel the desire to do lots of work with Bear, you may wish to get a small carved bear fetish or a picture to help your conscious mind have a more direct link to bears.

Pay attention to Bear when she appears in your dreams, and listen to the message she brings. Bears are always working in the dreamtime, especially during hibernation, when they are doing their trance work. If you dream of a bear, it is time to take this journey.

Your first visit to Eawokka is an introduction. You will have an opportunity to get a sense of the possibilities of Bear as ally and teacher, so that when you return you can bring specific questions. When working with Bear plan lengthy visits, for she has a lot to share and is willing to spend quite a long time.

A very slow, steady drumbeat is helpful during this journey. You may wish to have someone drum for you or make a drum tape to accompany you.

Place your bare feet in the dirt whenever possible, to help you feel the rhythm of the earth.

Bear Journey

[*Proceed with the alchemy. . . .*]

Thoth points the way toward the home of Bear, in the dark, cold realm of the North. You find yourself on a well-trodden path in a distant land of ice and crystals, a mountainous terrain. The path is part way up the side of a river valley and winds around a hill, terminating at the mouth of her cave. Pause and listen. . . . You can hear Eawokka inside. She is moving in a rocking motion back and forth, side to side, drumming—boom . . . boom . . . boom . . .—to put you in touch with the heartbeat of Gaia, Mother Earth. Listen. . . . Allow yourself to come into resonance with the pulse of the Mother. . . . Feel it in your cells and in your bones. . . . Feel it through your feet. . . . [*Long pause.*]

When you feel the pulse throughout your whole being, silently call out the name of Eawokka three times, and she will amble out of her cave to greet you. . . .

Notice the medallion Eawokka wears around her neck. She might let you climb on her back and hold the strap of the medallion like reins, or you may walk with her as she leads you to a pristine lake not far from her cave. She may nudge you a little to get you to jump into the icy cold water. The shocking sensation you feel when you immerse yourself stimulates a very deep level of your being. Although you are back out of the water in an instant, the effect lingers, and you have received a powerful purification.

Eawokka now takes you on a journey to begin to set the parameters of your relationship. She may take you into the forest to gather herbs, or she may invite you into her home for tea and to share with you her crystals and the knowledge of how to use them. Bear also knows the gateways to the stars. Allow her to connect with you in the deep and profound way that is especially available for you at this time. . . . [*Long pause to complete this experience. . . .*]

Eawokka takes you back to a very deep part of her cave, where the roof is full of crystals that are growing naturally. It is damp and cold, and water is dripping from the ceiling. Often she will take a crystal from the ceiling and give it to you to work with on your own healing process.

You may wish to give her a gift to help sustain her in her work. . . .

When your time is complete, follow the path back to where Thoth awaits to spend some time with you, sharing this experience. . . .

[*Thoth will assist you back into your body. Be sure to ground and center. . . .*]

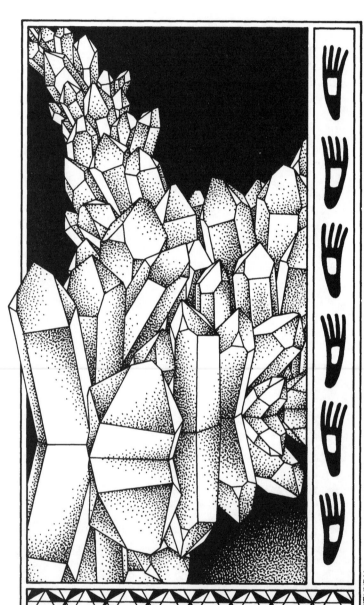

WERNEKE © 1991

CRYSTALS
Meditation

Everyone loves crystals for their beauty, their energy, and the ease with which they communicate with us. They have become extremely popular as tools for healing and consciousness development, yet many people have lost sight of the sacred nature and true value of these minerals. The mining industry that has developed to supply these and the crystals used in computer technology is depleting vast hidden veins of these beautiful and powerful natural resources.

The first structure of all creation was crystalline in nature. It is presumptuous for us to think that *we* are using *them,* for they are our elders and teachers, our ancestors. Crystals have been honored universally by indigenous peoples throughout time. The history of our planet is encapsulated within quartz crystals and can be read by sensitive seers.

There are many possibilities for working with crystals as allies. They amplify our thoughts and prayers and focus our intention. They can also be programmed to radiate frequencies encoded with intention to protect, heal, and hold the energy of rituals and ceremonies.

While they are buried in the earth crystals are doing a vital part in keeping Mother Earth alive. When they are dynamite blasted and bulldozed from the earth, they require special care. One of the things you can do to heal these crystals is to cleanse them, helping remove trauma. This can be accomplished in a number of ways: Rinse them in a clean, fast-moving stream; soak them overnight or for several days in sea salt and water, setting the bowl out in the elements so the crystals are touched by sunlight, moonlight, rain, and snow; take them to the ocean for a rinse. You can even bury them back in the earth for a period of time.

Crystals that are ready to be used are those that are washed up in the spring thaws or are lightly dug from the earth's surface. Some have worked their way up from the underworld. With a little effort, beautiful crystals can still be found quite easily, all over the world.

I offer the following journey in the hope that discovering the power of inner work with crystals will alleviate the need for continuing their unbridled harvest. This crystal cave is a place where one can return for meditation and receive inspiration and revitalization. It is not necessary to always take crystals. It is never acceptable to enter this cave without asking permission of the bear who is its guardian.

People who are facing great emotional or physical dis-ease can take this journey, and their whole being can become revitalized by the gleaming light of the sparkling crystals, a natural matrix similar to the Mother's womb. It brings solace to those who are suffering. Spend considerable time here to receive wisdom, knowledge, and information.

Crystal Journey

[*Do the Cauldron alchemy. . . .*]

Thoth is there, at your left. With him is a bear. This bear guides you to the entrance of a cave that is well camouflaged—it would be invisible if you were not shown. This place could be anywhere in the world. The initial opening passageway goes downward before giving way to a gigantic cavern with many rooms. The sound of dripping water echoes, as though fragmented by thousands of facets protruding from the vaulted ceiling. All of the surfaces sparkle. At first, the source of the glittering light is vague, presenting a mysterious, almost eerie glow.

Move to a place deeper in the cave where a natural chimney hole allows sunlight to shine directly onto the surface of the walls. Now you can see more clearly that you are surrounded by glittering crystals and gems, whose myriad facets reflect the light, all of which comes from the same source. The ceiling and walls are covered with crystals and gems of all shapes, colors, and sizes. Some of the chambers are geodes, like cracked-open eggs exhibiting dazzling crystal erectiles. Crystals are nestled in the roots and root fiber of massive trees that are growing above the cavern, on top of the earth. Some are in small rivulets of water washing down from above, lining the floor with loose crystals. Where these small rivers converge is a pool of clear, ice-cold water, approximately two feet deep, full of every type of crystal and gem imaginable.

Stand or kneel beside the edge of the pool. Open your heart and ask permission to remove some of the crystals from the sacred water. You must promise to respect and treat them with honor and to use them for the benefit and the healing of the planet and all who dwell upon her. . . .

The crystals that are to work with you will float to the surface. Offer a prayer of thanks for the gifts you have been given, and receive instructions for their use. . . . [*Long pause.*]

Spend some time in meditation in this cave sanctuary. There is amazing energy here, where you are surrounded by thousands of crystals and gems. You can receive a tremendous boost of emotional and physical healing as well as great enlightenment. Stay as long as it feels comfortable. . . . [*Long pause.*]

It is appropriate to leave a personal offering here, a piece of fingernail or some hair. . . .

When you are ready to leave, either ride on or walk next to your bear as she escorts you out of the cave. Be sure to thank your bear guide. Bears love sweet things like honey cakes or berries.

Return to where Thoth waits and spend a moment with him, discussing the cave and your relationship with crystals. . . .

[*Thoth will assist you back into your body.* . . .]

WERNEKE © 1991

Gold
Energy

The spirit of Gold is very, very ancient. It has been revered from time immemorial as the physical manifestation of the sun, the source of all life. Gold was forged early in the creation of our physical universe. It can be melted, cast, hammered paper thin, or made into liquid. It can be alloyed and compounded. Although it is one of the most malleable of all minerals, it is unchangeable and incorruptible.

Many wars have been fought over its possession, for gold is a sign of wealth. Throughout history, it has adorned the bodies of the rich, and churches and temples throughout the world reflect the sun off their shining gold mantles. Gold reflects the spirit of the wearer, whose greed or spirituality is evident to anyone who chooses to notice.

Gold is a healer and protector of the earth, and these are the aspects that Gold wishes to share in the Cauldron teachings. The awareness that gold has medicinal value is not new. For example, it is a common remedy for arthritis in both allopathic and homeopathic medical systems, and it is a radionic reagent for the heart. When you use gold medicinally, it must be pure, as must be your intentions when you ask the spirit of Gold to assist you after you have taken this journey.

Within the earth's system, there is a very delicate vibrational balance between all of the elements, minerals, and compounds. By mining out any one of these and moving it to another location on the planet or dispersing it, a change is made in the vibrational flows throughout the planet. The original ecological balance is disrupted. The spirit of Gold has the ability to influence the more mobile entities in its field into doing things that would help build a new balance. These entities include plants, animals, and people. Gold and quartz enjoy working with the other kingdoms, especially humans, more so than most of the other minerals do. Quartz is gold's natural ally and is often found in close proximity to it.

The vibratory rate of gold is very slow in comparison to the rate of animals. For humans to understand something like a rock or a metal, they have to change their vibratory rate enough so that they can begin to resonate with that particular mineral and communicate with it. In order to give you that experience, Gold's journey takes you deep into Earth. If you find that after this journey you feel somewhat stuck or overly grounded, try an air journey like Hawk or Eagle, or explore air with Lion.

Gold Journey

[*Do the alchemy. . . .*]
Thoth is there and helps you back into your body in such a way that you maintain your light-body state. . . . Breathe in through the small of your back and then out and downward, into the earth. Each expulsion of breath takes you deeper. Through breathing in this way, your consciousness passes through different types and layers of minerals and soil as you descend deeper and deeper. . . .

With the exhale of your fifth breath, you reach a vein of gold. . . . Continue to breathe in this way as your exhales take you further into this vein. It is very large, and soon your entire consciousness is surrounded by gold. . . . As you breathe, you can smell the metal of this brilliant, glowing, yellow mineral. You are able to distinguish it in your own body by your senses. Identify it and realize that the feeling of this gold is very different from the feeling of the earth, the soil. It feels like a metal. It feels yellow. It feels hard. It conducts electricity in such a way that you can feel unusual currents going through your body.

Breathe in the feeling of the gold until your entire body is full, so you feel the same inside as you feel outside. Through your body, notice the minute electrical currents that this gold is conducting.

As you look closely at the gold in front of your eyes, you are able to see into it in a way that you couldn't before. It no longer looks or feels solid. You can see its metallic, molecular structures. As you look at these basic building components, you can see that they're made up of many smaller components. You can see the energy currents and the particles running from one part of the structure to another in a way that is purposeful rather than random. You can feel these electrical messages on the inside of your body as well as on the outside, and you become aware of the inner communication of one particle and structure with another.

As you expand your view, the gold looks like a giant city lit up at night, with little lights traveling as far as you can see in every direction. There is an overall intelligence and purpose governing all this energy and these lights. . . .

As you breathe deeply, you become aware of a more solid gold substance all around and inside you. There is a sensation deep inside your being with which you have become acquainted, and you are now able to speak with the spirit of the mineral in whose home you are a guest. Listen now to the knowledge of the mineral gold. . . . [*Long pause.*]

You now have the opportunity to ask some questions of the spirit of Gold. . . . [*Long pause.*]

Be sure to thank this spirit and make an offering of energy. . . .

To return, take five deep breaths, breathing in through the small of your back, and with each exhale, propelling yourself back upward into your human consciousness. . . .

Take a moment to share this experience with Thoth. . . .

[*Thoth touches your crown and you are back in ordinary consciousness, in your physical form.* . . .]

WERNEKE © 1991

DEER

Sensitivity

Deer are wonderful guides with many attributes. They have an incredible capacity to hear and can teach you to listen. They are also very compassionate; there is always opportunity for mending when the gentle, soft deer is in your life. Deer are extremely watchful, with keen wariness. Think of the deer with great big brown eyes, watching, watching. . . . They have the ability to perceive threats—sniffing danger, yet moving with grace, agility, and care in peaceful communion with nature. Deer have sharp hearing and clairvoyant sight, and they are able to move instinctively and make quick decisions, disappearing like a shadow when chased. They live for the joy of the moment. Deer are also a symbol of longevity, their horns growing anew each year symbolize regeneration.

The best way to take the journey of the deer is to dance physically. You may wish to empower a shawl, piece of cloth, or animal hide so that whenever you put it on you commit to bringing in the power of the deer. Often kinesthetic people benefit from having an antler or piece of antler to touch. A picture can also be used to invoke Deer.

During different times of the year, you may experience different phases or aspects of deer life, in accordance with the season and your immediate needs. You may be a yearling, a buck during rutting season, or a pregnant doe.

It is helpful to have a tambourine or rattle to enhance the rhythm, the sense of fleetness required to help you move with the deer through the deer's world. Allow yourself plenty of time to get used to the dance. It's especially wonderful to experience this journey outdoors in a natural setting.

Deer Journey

[*Do the alchemy. . . .*]

When you come out of the Cauldron for the deer journey, Thoth is there wearing animal skins, holding a rattle, and looking very much like a shaman. You also are dressed in skins—deer skins. Thoth begins to dance, initiating the rhythm to which you also begin to dance.

As you and Thoth dance together, you transform into a deer. Notice the changes in your body and consciousness as you get into the spirit of being a deer. As you become comfortable moving in your deer body, everything seems gentle and peaceful within nature. The green of the shrubs and bushes stands out. Smell the scent of the pines and the wild roses. The tips and shoots of green leaves are delectable, especially the young tips of evergreen trees. You are in tune with each step you take and with the sound your cloven hooves make as they touch the ground.

It is through your heart that you feel this experience. Notice the connection between your heart and your ears, as though you can hear with your heart. Listen to the sounds of the forest you love. If there is a sound that doesn't belong, you smell to figure out what it is. You also smell your deer friends to keep track of where they are. . . .

Nimbly yet stealthily, you find your way to a stream, drawn by the scent of the water and your ability to hear its babbling call. There is a clear pool where the water is caught by a tangle of rocks and mossy fallen trees. As you reach for the cool, sweet water, your reflection is one of beauty and gentleness. Gazing at yourself as Deer, you realize how much you belong to the forest. You are a guardian of the purity of nature, of the freedom that comes through living in tune with the natural harmony of the forest. . . . [*Pause.*]

Drink your fill of the pure water, and take off on an exploration of your domain. Notice how your senses have sharpened, how fleet-footed you have become, and how swiftly you can alter your course. You are instinctively in tune with those who are in your environment, knowing who is harmless and who is not.

As you look out through the eyes of Deer, receive a further teaching about living in harmony with yourself in your environment. . . .

When you feel complete with this experience, return to the clearing where Thoth and your physical form are still dancing. Your consciousness leaves the deer and enters your human form.

As you look back at the deer, she gazes upon you with the pure innocence of the virgin forest that is her home. Deer asks you to remember to step in pure harmony with the forest and mountain spirits. Offer a gift of sustenance to the deer and your respect for the trust that you see in her unspoiled eyes. . . . With a flick of her tail, she leaves.

Discuss with Thoth how this ally will continue to work with you.

[*Thoth assists you back into your body through your crown.* . . .]

KUAN YIN
Healing/Compassion

All people will benefit from the healing journey with Kuan Yin. She has been worshiped as the Chinese bodhisattva of compassion by millions of people for thousands of years. She is known to be one of the most accessible entities; her name means "She-Who-Hearkens-to-the-Cries-of-the-World." Individuals from all walks of life, from fisherfolk and Buddhist laymen to Taoist sages, venerate her as a goddess of mercy. (For further information, see *Bodhisattva of Compassion,* by John Blofeld. Boston: Shambhala, 1988.)

In Tibet, Kuan Yin is known as Tara. In Christian cultures she corresponds most closely with Mother Mary. She is called "Kwannon Sama" in Japan and is as popular there as she is in China.

In response to the suffering throughout our planet, especially from the raging epidemics of AIDS, leukemia, and other terminal diseases, Kuan Yin offered the following journey into the Cauldron. It can be effective for those with a wide range of physical and emotional problems.

In this journey, you find yourself in an ancient landscape of peace and tranquillity. There you will meet Kuan Yin to receive healing and guidance and to have an opportunity to reach a deeper understanding of your disease and the message it brings, as well as to learn about your healing process.

Kuan Yin Journey

[*When you have completed the alchemy, greet Thoth and request assistance with your healing process. . . .*]

It is early evening and a nightingale appears, silhouetted against the sky. Follow as it leads the way to a bridge that connects to an island in the middle of a wide river. As the nightingale flies over the bridge, follow on foot, and as you step onto the bridge, become aware that it is alive and that you are walking on the curved backbone of a dragon. The dragon twists its head out of the water and looks at you as you cross on its back. Its eyes are luminous pools of a liquid color. As you look deeply into its eyes, this dragon is knowing you. All the aspects of who and what you are are received and reflected in its mirrorlike eyes. . . . [*Pause.*] This dragon knows and accepts you without judgment and gives its blessing as you step onto the island of Kuan Yin.

There is a feeling of ancient China here. As your senses awaken to the delights of this garden, you can smell the air of a lush and fragrant summer evening.

As you move toward the center of the island, there is an open Chinese temple. A presence patiently waits for you, and as you walk toward the inward glade, you can see the pale, calm, luminous face of Kuan Yin. Her hair is caught up on her head with gold hair ornaments that make a tinkling sound when she moves. She is dressed in rich silk robes. She appears small. Loving, gentle, and welcoming, she greets you by placing a hand on her heart, then holding it out for your hand. She's delighted to be with you.

Kuan Yin looks at your face and your body, and you feel throughout your being her loving acceptance of who you are. She is able to see your true beauty unveiled and not clouded by the earthly realm. She begins to move her hands around and through your body, clearing and healing any dark places and filling every cell of your body with her love.

Any diseased cells cannot accept this bounty, and Kuan Yin picks them out very easily and places them in a bowl. They might look like black lumps of coal. As she removes them, you are able to study them from an objective view, and you feel your fears and self-doubts also depart until they are no longer a part of you. . . . [*Long pause.*]

Follow Kuan Yin as she carries the bowl to the river's edge, where the dragon awaits. . . . As she holds up the bowl, the dragon breathes the fire of wisdom, burning everything in the bowl quickly away. As you perceive the smoke rising to the sky and dissipating in the breeze, go within yourself and search for understanding. Kuan Yin is there in all compassion to help you heal yourself; she cherishes every part of your being. So be with yourself and Kuan Yin as you seek to know the changes you must make to complete this healing. . . . [*Long pause.*]

Kuan Yin now leads you to a pool. Take off the clothes you are wearing and step into the cool, clear water. She pours water over you from a vessel, cleansing you, and in this way you are reborn, clean and fresh. You feel a great joy and happiness in living. Kuan Yin shares this with you.

She gives you a gift, a token that is a protective amulet of a green color. She tells you to call her whenever you want. You can invite her presence by using the token she has given you.

Spend the next few moments with Kuan Yin, continuing to receive her healing and further suggestions she might give you at this time.

When you feel complete, follow the nightingale as she flies back over the dragon bridge.

Thoth is waiting on the other side. Recount your experience to him. . . .

[*Thoth will assist you back into your body. . . .*]

WERNEKE © 1991

GOLDEN EAGLE
Family Relationships/Codependency

Golden Eagles are regal birds, admired for their size, power, and magnificent flying capabilities. Like people, they are a top predator, for although they eat other animals, they are seldom hunted for food. Thus, they help to keep balance in the natural world.

Golden Eagle brought this journey into the Cauldron to help you develop better family relationships, especially concerning codependent behavior. In this journey, a golden eagle will assist you in better understanding your own family unit by demonstrating eagle family life. Eagles mate for life, and they share parental duties. They function as a unit yet also independently. Although mated, eagles do not require their partner to be at their side every minute of the day. This journey will also help you learn that you can fly just as well alone as with another.

This is a reprogramming, a renurturing, for you will be literally an egg in an eagle's nest, then a hatchling, and then raised very quickly into adult eaglehood, so that you get the balancing of both the male and the female parent and gain a role model for family life. This reprogramming allows you to erase only the negative patterns you have witnessed or experienced in your past. If you need special healing with regard to finding a mate, this is a good journey to use as a practice, and you can also work with Swan. If you have trouble with the courting and mating part of the journey, or if you are simply not ready to deal with that part, return at a later time and work with it again until you achieve appropriate resolution.

Your experience will span time, similar to time-lapse photography.

Eagles gestate for up to fifty days. It often takes thirty-five to forty hours for them to hatch out of their shells. You will be doing this much faster in your journey.

Following is a special alchemy you need to use in order to prepare yourself to become a golden eagle.

Golden Eagle Journey

Ground and center with your breath and place your hands before you to receive a golden egg. . . . Take the golden egg into your abdomen and leave it resting gently, gestating in your Golden Cauldron. . . . Kindle the flame within your heart with your love, and bask in the radiance and warmth of its light. . . . As you stir the water in the Cauldron, it rises to meet the fire in your heart center, carrying the egg upward. Place your attention and consciousness within the golden egg as it floats up with the steam and is carried out through your crown. . . . Thoth guides your egg safely to the nest. You do not see him, but you are aware of his presence. . . .

Pay attention to the feeling of being inside the egg and what sounds you hear through the shell. Can you feel the warmth of the eagle that sits on the eggs? As you stretch and move around, notice how you feel. As you grow, the space seems smaller, tighter, more cramped. You feel yourself pressing against the sides of your shell until you have nowhere to go. As you struggle to free yourself from the confines of gestation, you discover that you have a special "egg tooth" on your beak to crack your shell and break off the first chip from the inside. You must work harder to break out of the shell completely. No one helps you with this process. . . . [*Long pause.*]

When you finally emerge, notice the light, any smells, how your body structure feels, the wetness of your feathers drying in the fresh air and sun. Your voice squeaks as you cry out to celebrate the victory of your birth.

Rest for a moment, letting your feathers dry and begin to fluff. . . . Experience your first meal. How is it given to you? What does it taste like?

Your parents take turns guarding the nest, which is quite high, perched in a crook at the top of an ancient conifer skeleton. How do they respond to your needs? Notice all of the details of your first months as an eaglet. . . . [*Long pause.*]

It is time to experience flight. No one has brought you food for some time, and you are very hungry. Your mother flies by with a big chunk of salmon. At first it appears that she is bringing it to the nest, but she is only teasing. She returns and flaunts the luscious morsel again, taunting you. The next time she flies by, lean out of your nest and try to grab a bite. Stretch yourself, holding tight to the nest with your talons, reaching for the salmon. A twig breaks away from the nest and you lose your balance and fall toward the ground. Quickly you reach out your wings to steady yourself and catch the wind that picks you up again.

It takes some doing, but you find your natural abilities for flying without too much effort. As you soar above your habitat, your keen sight focuses on the landscape far below where a rabbit (or other appropriate food source) scurries across an open space looking for cover. Let yourself experience the dive as you swoop down and capture your prey with sharp talons. For the first time in your eagle life you have provided for yourself. Enjoy the meal. . . .

Time passes quickly, and soon you are ready to find a mate. . . . Observe your courting and mating process. . . .

When the cycle has been completed, you return to your body by looking for the golden egg that, for this journey, signifies your crown. Thoth will be there to help you enter your physical body as Eagle, bringing back with you all the reencodements of your experience. Take a moment to reflect upon this experience with Thoth. . . .

[*Once back in your human form, your experience as Eagle is integrated as part of you. Ground and center. . . .*]

Frog

Cleansing

Anyone who has collected frog jelly, the little black eggs in the gelatinous substance found in stagnant ponds in springtime, knows that, when put in water, this jelly becomes tadpoles. They miraculously begin to develop legs and soon turn into amphibian frogs. Because of this process, Frog is a major symbol of transformation and metamorphosis.

Where he appears in mythology, Frog evokes either great respect or revulsion. Stone figures of frogs were found in the mouths of the dead in ancient burial grounds of the Chinese and the Mayans, for whom Frog is a reincarnation symbol. These frog fetishes were made of jade in China and of other stones in the New World. Egypt's gentle goddess of childbirth and fertility, Heket, had the head or the entire form of a frog.

Associations with rain are attributed to Frog primarily in India and South America. Lowland Mayan and Olmec tribes identified Frog with water, mucous, and semen, as well as with rain for crops and the continued growth of the forest. The Huron tribe of North America and the aborigines of Queensland, Australia, have similar myths about frogs swallowing all the water in times of drought. In Australia, the water was released by making the frog laugh, a feat accomplished by the eel, whose squirming and wriggling antics made the frog roar with laughter. For the Hurons, it was Ioskeha, the creation hero, who stabbed the frog, releasing all of the water from the frog's belly.

The myth of the frog prince relates to Frog's ability to perceive the true soul, the highest potential of everyone, which usually happens through the transformative power of love.

Indispensable to our forests, frogs are very magical creatures who call in the rain. When you have frog medicine, you can also work with water to cleanse negative energies. Use water in any healing work you do. You can put water in your mouth and spray in onto your altar. When you do a healing, you can spray it out over the person, envisioning that the spray comes from, the frogs, to clear negative energy. Be sure to picture the frogs and hold the notion of cleansing for your altar or healing while you do this, so that the effect will be a blessing rather than a profanity. (Spraying in a similar manner is practiced in several cultures, including those of South America and Africa, and might not be directly associated with Frog. In Africa, for example, spraying is empowering and is done by a person whose mouth has gone through rituals. Totemically it would be more closely related to Elephant, whose spray is considered sacred.)

Frogs are an indicator species in the ecosystem, calling our attention to the health of the environment. Many species of frogs have vanished mysteriously in recent years, suggesting a relationship to environmental conditions similar to that of the canary to the coal mine. This is a critical situation, for all things in nature evolve and work together. Where frogs are disappearing, it may indicate pollution in ground, water, and air.

Frogs bring the rain, and with the rain comes cleansing. Their call is not a cry of desperation but, rather, an acknowledgment honoring the waters of life.

In the Cauldron, Frog teaches us how to cleanse negative energy and reminds us of the value of our forests. This journey can be enhanced by acting it out physically. Try sitting like a frog and even hopping about like one. You can visit Frog while taking a shower or bath if you'd like. Go ahead and make it fun and playful. Make lots of noise! Children will love this one, and it works well as a group activity.

Frog Journey

[*Do the alchemy. . . .*]
Thoth directs you to a lush, green forest. It is so rich and verdant that it takes a moment to realize that the ground is covered with frogs—they are everywhere. As they begin to croak, a rhythm develops. More and

more frogs join the chorus, adding their unique rhythm to the song they are creating. The powerful sound comes from their guts and calls forth the rain with love. . . .

As you continue to resonate with the sound of the frogs, feel yourself become one, noticing the vibration that wells up from your own gut as you add your voice to the cry for rain. You vocalize a "r-i-b-i-t" that is audible and felt throughout the entire front underside of your body, completing your transfiguration into Frog. . . .

Look down and notice your webbed feet and your spotted amphibian legs. Your eyes bulge as you continue to "r-i-b-i-t." Go ahead and catch a fly that happens to pass within range. Swallow it. You might not see the other frogs around at this point, but you know they are there by the resonance of the sound. The sound becomes more and more powerful. It lifts the vibration in the forest and contacts the water spirits above, resulting in rain. . . .

Feel the rain as it falls, and continue to make your sounds. The water of the rain is cleansing. You can hear it dripping from the trees, snaking into puddles all around you. The voice of Frog calls attention to an area of your body or life that most needs the healing from the rains. Perceive the cleansing effect of the rain as it extends to your own body, mind, and psyche. . . . [*Long pause.*]

As an offering, use the space that you have created to cleanse some area in your life or to send cleansing, healing energies to another person. . . .
You may also consider what you can do to help the forest so that the frogs have a place to reproduce. . . .

To return, jump up, and you're back in your human form with Thoth, who may be holding an umbrella! Take time to discuss the possibilities of this work in your life. . . .

[*Thoth will assist you back. . . .*]

Part **VI**

JOURNEYS FOR
EXPLORATION

In this section, you can stretch out and play. If you have become an intrepid traveler, you can uncover some very deep knowledge about yourself and the creation within which you express life and consciousness.

HAWK

Illumination

Hawk is a raptor, intent and focused. In Egypt, Hawk is Horus, the divine son of the birth goddess, Isis, and her husband, Osiris, god of death and the fecund earth. Horus represents our highest aspect, and his eye is the eye of the sun, which illumines all things. As the reflection of our highest selves, he is all seeing, all knowing, all being. He helps us aspire to our goals in accordance with our highest potential.

As the divine child, Horus is also the initiated one. He is a protector of life and the sacred ways, one who provides inspiration. The eye of Horus shines light through the darkness of infinite space, giving us clear vision to see through all dimensions into the essence of things.

Horus's father, Osiris, was slain by his jealous brother, Set. Isis found him, even though Set had cut him up and scattered the fourteen pieces throughout Egypt. With the help of Thoth, she was able to put him back together, with the exception of his phallus, which had been thrown into the Nile and devoured. The phallus was re-created in wood and used to conceive Horus. Horus grew to be a fine warrior, the avenger of his father, and engaged in a lengthy and violent battle with Set over the throne of Osiris. Eventually Horus was declared the victor by the pantheon of the gods.

Hawk is a noble helper who sees with great clarity and profound vision. Through the perspective of Hawk, you can look to the origins of a present problem or plan. Use your intent and ask Hawk to review with you aspects of your immediate, current life so that you can find a new way of perceiving your situation. Experiencing this new clarity of vision will be like lifting the hood of a falcon, who goes directly for what is targeted. With Hawk, you can see whatever you've missed or ignored. You can also distinguish that which nourishes you from that which would bring you harm.

This journey is also useful for looking back to your origins to find your purpose for this lifetime. It is best to have your aspirations in mind before you start so that you are clear and definitive when you communicate with Hawk.

Following are three possible journeys with Hawk. The first has to do with viewing a current situation in your life. The second allows you to explore your past, either in this or another lifetime. Studying past lives can be helpful when you are able to find resolution for by relating them to current conditions or situations by relating them to experiences of the past. The third is a journey of the heart that helps you perceive the possibilities of your future.

Hawk Journeys

Present

[*Do the alchemy. . . .*]

When you get to Thoth, ask to see Hawk. Thoth raises his ankh, the key of life, to the sun. Allow for hope to grow in your heart as you call forth Hawk to see life in a new way. Offer him a branch, a place to rest, by holding out your left arm for him to rest upon as you allow your own intention, hope, and will to develop.

Hawk drops out of the sun, and you feel his weight as he lands on your hand. You can feel his talons digging into your wrist or forearm. He has small, sharp claws and a curved beak. As you look into the eye of Hawk, focus from your heart on what you've chosen to look at, and according to your simple and clear, from-the-heart intent, Hawk will show you what you may be missing, what is important for you to focus on. He will shed new light upon your immediate goals, and this new perception—the sharp, clear vision of the hawk—will allow you access to change. According to your own clear heart intention, his light will illuminate whatever you want to see. . . .

Give yourself time to experience the necessary changes. . . . [*Long pause.*] Hawk will stay with you as your intention connects you back to your own day-to-day life.

[*Thoth will be there to assist you back into your body. . . .*]

Past

You can also journey with Hawk into your past, whether in this or another lifetime, to see who you've been, where you are now, and where you could be going in your life. Hawk can take you back to your origins so that you can better understand your purpose in this life. It is possible to travel back to Atlantis, Lemuria, or another land to receive a teaching [*Follow the preceding instructions, calling Hawk down from the sun. . . .*]

When Hawk has landed on your outstretched arm, make your request to experience your origins or a past life as you look deeply into his eye. You are taken to an experience from your past that is relevant to your present life. . . . [*Long pause.*]

When this experience is complete, Horus will bring you back to Thoth. Take a moment to share with him. . . .

[*Thoth assists you back into your body. . . .*]

Future

[*Do the Cauldron alchemy, and call Hawk. . . .*]

Open your heart to your hawk friend, and as you make your heart connection, he lifts his wings to create the shape of a heart. Pass through the heart-shaped door. . . . Horus carries you beyond your earthly past and out into space, where you are given a teaching about how all things are connected in the universe. . . . [*Pause.*]

Eventually, you are brought to a landscape of peaceful rivers and valleys through which you fly until you enter a serene, beautiful sanctuary with water flowing in a fountain or stream and many fruits and flowers. In this lush, well-tended place you can calm your thoughts and find peace of mind. Here you are given a vision of all the changes that are required in order to achieve your future goals. . . . [*Long pause.*]

As you return, it is as though you are flying through all the possibilities that exist on your future path. . . . [*Long pause.*]

Hawk brings you back to Thoth. Share your experience with him. . . .

[*Thoth assists you back into your body. . . .*]

LIONESS

Elemental Kingdoms

Lioness represents self-assuredness. She stands for action, authority, divine strength, and courage. In ancient Egypt, Sekhmet, the lion-headed warrior goddess, reigned as guardian and avid protectoress of Maät, goddess of truth and justice. Her wrath, when irked, is almost unquenchable, yet she is a great ally, capable of immeasurable compassion.

To be in the presence of Sekhmet, as either goddess or lion, is to feel the power and strength of one who sees and acts with absolute discernment and intelligence. Her proud essence helps establish well-being wherever she goes. It is not Sekhmet but rather the totemic African Lioness who appears in the following Cauldron journey. If you wish to meet Sekhmet, you must travel a different way. After you become comfortable with Lioness, you can ask Thoth to take you to Egypt to meet Sekhmet at her temple.

The African Lioness embodies the same attributes as Sekhmet and brings many gifts into the Cauldron. Lions are the undisputed monarchs of the wild creatures of Africa. Their skins are worn by tribespeople when they dance to acquire courage and cunning for the hunt and for battle. This Cauldron journey is a hunt for knowledge and experience about the elements, a study of vital interest to anyone trying to comprehend the nature of reality. Westerners commonly consider earth, water, fire, and air to be the basic four elements.

Understanding these elements can be very helpful in modulating your physical health and behavioral characteristics, for when they are balanced in your body and mind, all things are in order and will function harmoniously. Too much or too little of an element will disrupt bodily functions or change patterns of behavior.

The Cauldron journey with Lioness takes you to the elementals, the spirits of the kingdoms of Earth, Water, Fire, and Air. You travel to these realms in an open-ended journey in which Lioness helps you with your hunt, for when you go to elemental realms it is helpful to go with an experienced hunter. While looking through the eyes of Lioness or being in the companionship of Lioness, you can travel safely to any of the elemental kingdoms. Her watchful sight and sound judgment will help you see what is the most personally beneficial aspect of that realm. For example, if you go to the Fire kingdom, Lioness's clear vision and stalking ability will lead you to an experience of fire, during which you may face searing heat as it burns away weakness to bring you to recognize your inherent courage.

The intelligent denizens of the elemental kingdoms will always appear as distinctive entities, creatures of the nature of the specific element that you are exploring. In the Earth kingdom, you might work with dwarfs, elves, and Earth beings. In water, you might find undines or water sprites. In Fire, spirits are often salamanders, and in Air you encounter fairies and sylphs.

When you travel on this hunting expedition with Lioness, you choose the element you want to explore. Her intelligence looks for the best advantage, so that you can discover what is happening for you in your realm of interest. Lioness is an opportunistic hunter, and you are protected in each realm by her steadfast qualities of fierceness, unwavering courage, and strength.

There are many types of feeding and nourishment available through your travels with Lioness. Sometimes she drinks water or eats a large or a small animal. Sometimes lions play with each other or with the cubs, and they enjoy playing with their food. That's how these journeys go—they're not just for food, but for fun and curiosity as well.

Choose which element you plan to visit before you take the journey, and use the direction that is given to enter through its doorway. The entry/exit place to these realms is a portal that has the general characteristics of the element.

Earth

As you travel across the veld to get into Earth, the landscape becomes more dense. You pass through an area of heavy growth that terminates suddenly, at a place where earth and rocks join in a rugged rise that is broken by cliffs and chasms. Your lioness knows where she is going and takes you to a narrow crevice that enters directly into Earth. . . .

Once in the Earth kingdom, you may be introduced to Earth entities such as dwarfs, elves, trolls, gnomes, or other earthy beings. They are the guardians of the mineral kingdom and the treasures of Earth. Here you can learn about physical healing and the attributes of this element. Earthy people are grounded and physical in orientation. Conservative, stable, constructive, organized, determined, and solid are catchwords that describe Earth characteristics.

Water

The watery entities, including undines and water sprites, can be found in or around water. The portal to that kingdom can be a stream, a lake or large body of water, a waterfall, or a mountain pool. The journey in the Water realm can be in marshes, on the shore, or deep in the world of feelings, emotions, dreams, or fantasy. Water is the mirror world, revealing your needs, desires, and illusions. Travel with your lioness to find a clear, sacred pool and dive through its surface into the realm of Water. Explore emotions, psychic awareness, intuition, and compassion. Watery people tend to be nurturing, sensitive, and, sometimes, secretive.

Fire

A volcano or other fiery place will offer entrance to the kingdom of Fire, or your lioness might leap through bright, flickering flames. Notice the feeling of the element: the warmth, the quickness, the fascination. Fire might be found in woods or fields. Its inhabitants look like elves or fairies, but they are flaming, vibrating. Or you might meet a salamander.

In Fire, you can develop passion and the creative power of your will. It is the realm of spirit. Fiery people tend to be courageous and aggressive, and too much fire can result in anger, rage or even violence. By working within an element that is out of balance, you can learn how to bring it back into equilibrium.

Air

The Air world is reached by climbing to great heights with expansive vistas, even up into the sky or clouds. The entrance might be a leap across a great chasm, altering your spatial perspective. You may encounter winged fairies, sylphs, or flying, soaring entities like Phoenix or Eagle. In the Air kingdom, you learn about communication and ideas and can obtain information about the mind and humor. Song and poetry are often inspired here, as this is the element of the Muses. Airy people tend to be idealistic, intellectual, lighthearted, abstract, and funny, and Air is the realm to visit to "lighten up" or expand your consciousness.

In each of the realms, Lioness's attention will locate a being who may wait for, approach, or greet you. It is important when traveling in the elemental kingdoms to hold your own. Being with Lioness provides additional strength and protection. If your reason for being there is specific, tell the entity, and he or she will lead you to your goal. Otherwise, let the elemental being lead you to whatever information or experience is appropriate.

Each time you go to a realm, you will have an experience specific to your needs or desire, and then you will be brought back by your lioness guide to the resting area on the veld.

Traveling with these majestic felines brings understanding. Each time you return to this journey, it will be different.

Lioness Journey

[*Refer to the elements in the introduction to Lioness, and choose which elemental kingdom you wish to explore. Go through the Cauldron alchemy to Thoth.*]

Thoth takes you to the veld in Africa where the lions live. There, by the side of a river or watering hole, you will see a pride of lions lazing about in the afternoon sun. The heat of the day is sweltering, almost oppressive, as you tune more clearly into the lions' space. The stillness is broken only by tails switching to keep the incessant insects away.

One of the lions catches your eye. As you return her gaze, greet Lioness. From your heart, request the information or experience you need, and Lioness will rise to take you on a hunt. You must distinguish which elemental kingdom you want to explore and express any specific purpose you might have.

Lioness invites you into her body, yet you maintain your own separate consciousness. . . . As she takes off across the veld at an easy lope, feel the power of her movements, the rhythm of her muscles, as they pull her body through the motions that carry her easily and swiftly forward. Her senses are fully alert, yet she seems disinterested in the herds of animals you may pass, although some will scatter and run at the very sight of her. Pay attention to the landscape. She smells the wind and instinctively knows her direction. She pauses for a moment and lets out a rumbling growl. Notice where in your body the sound vibrates. . . . Lioness takes you to higher ground in search of an appropriate entrance to the element of your choice. . . .

Once you have entered that kingdom, retain your individual identity. You are taken to the appropriate elemental being and given the experience that will satiate your hunger for knowledge. . . . [*Long pause.*]

When your experience of the elemental kingdom of your choice is complete, Lioness will take you back into her body for the return trip, back the way you came. . . . She takes you to the veld, where the pride continues to rest by the watering hole.

Look into Lioness's eyes until you are at peace with this powerful creature. You feel satisfied and full, and you may wish to curl up with this ally and take a nap while you digest your meal of information or experience, just as lions normally do after they hunt. . . .

In time, Thoth will reappear. Recount your experience to him . . . .

[*Thoth will assist you back into your body.* . . .]

CEDAR TREE
Akasha

In the Cauldron, Cedar provides the gateway into the realm of Akasha, a domain of knowledge. Traditions differ in their element systems; some include Akasha as a fifth element, the medium from which the other four elements—earth, water, fire, and air—derive.

Akasha is equivalent to what some traditions call the "ethers," and it can be described as similar to the deep space of the night sky, spangled with stars. Its color is either indigo or the purple-black, flecked-with-gold color of the etheric egg in the Cauldron alchemy. The egg is a universal symbol of creation, and the two-dimensional representation of an egg—an oval—can be used as a portal into Akasha.

The symbol we will use to enter this realm is the *vesica piscis*, literally the vessel, or bladder, of the fish. The symbol is formed by the intersection of two circles, representing the "above" and the "below," and the central shape that is created becomes the symbol for Akasha. The cross section of a fish reveals the symbol; it is also the shape of the female yoni, or vulva.

There are many pathways to access the Akashic records, the etheric library where all past, present, and future knowledge is stored. In the Golden Cauldron, it is the ancient and gracious cedar tree that forms the doorway.

One of the oldest recorded myths in the world is a legend about the Babylonian goddess Ishtar, known to Sumerians as Inanna, whose throne was a giant cedar tree in a vast virgin forest. It is a patriarchal myth about the power in separation. The throne of Ishtar was guarded by the dragonlike monster known as Humbaba. Humbaba was a huge Earth guardian, part lion and part dragon, belching fire from his mouth.

Gilgamesh was a warrior, hero, and king, always restless and searching for a way to carve his name in stone. He was not well liked in the land where he lived, and his presence was feared, for he was a bully and womanizer before his transformation later in life. Gilgamesh was mortal, though two parts god and one part human, and the first to violate the forest. He sought to put his mark on the land by killing the evil giant that guarded the forest. He succeeded, and when Humbaba died, the magic of the forest became scattered in all directions—to the underworld, the streams, the trees. No longer was the magic the total fabric.

When Gilgamesh entered the forest, he and his cohorts followed the path that Humbaba used and found their way to the great-grandmother cedar tree that was the dwelling place of the Goddess, the throne of Ishtar. As if to make a statement of conquest, Gilgamesh swung his axe with all his might on the trunk of the majestic cedar. The wound that was created from the blow of the axe healed into the shape of the *vesica piscis*, and it is that doorway that we use for our access into the Akashic realm. The images used here are very different from most views of the Akashic records, as we are entering through the throne of the Goddess.

This is a place to go for knowledge, and it is helpful to have a specific question in mind. As you practice and become comfortable in the realm of Akasha, you will learn how to retrieve detailed information. It may take more than one journey to learn to maintain consciousness here, as it can be a very "spacy" experience. You will be told to retrieve a gift from the heart of the earth. It is important to take that gift with you, as it will help to keep you grounded so you don't float off and lose conscious memory of your experience.

Cedar boughs make excellent incense and are often used as a smudge for cleansing negative energies from places, people, or tools. To gather cedar in a sacred and respectful way, find the largest, oldest tree in the grove and make an offering of tobacco or cornmeal to the four directions. Tell the tree what you intend to do with its leaves and sprinkle your offering beneath its branches. Then gather what you need from smaller trees nearby.

Cedar Journey

[Do the Cauldron alchemy. . . .]

Thoth points the way to a massive virgin forest. You are in ancient Sumeria, now known as Iraq. This forest is immense. Lush coniferous evergreen trees, tall and stately, their feathery branches uplifted as though in prayer, extend in every direction, as far as the eye can see. You follow the track where Humbaba used to walk. The way is broad, and the going is easy.

It is not hard to find the glade where the giant cedar tree stands like a colossus in front of a green mountain in the heart of the forest. It is a magnificent tree with a huge girth, comparable to California redwoods. Her branches reach out as if to embrace the whole of nature, generating a feeling of comfort and compassion, security and nourishment. This cedar forms a real seat for the Goddess, towering above the rest of the forest and offering ample shade.

As you gaze upon this great-grandmother cedar, it is as though a golden, glowing rectangle is etched upon her trunk. Enter the tree through the rectangular door. Immediately, your consciousness expands to encompass your tree body. Let your attention rise up through the trunk and spread out through your branches. Extend your focus until you're in the very tips of the cedar and can envision the aura around each soft, feathery, new growth of needles. . . .

Take the time you need to move into the appropriate consciousness so that all your senses appreciate the experience. Smell the pungent juices; the aroma of cedar has a cleansing effect, and you can feel the release of negativity, doubt, and the pressures and tensions of your life. As the wind gently swirls through your branches, these things are carried away and your purification is completed. . . .

Center your awareness back within the heart of your tree. Feel the strength and flexibility of your trunk. Here you have a sense of the power that allows you to withstand the storms that inevitably pass through this magical forest. . . .

Move your consciousness down into the roots. Incredible energy is coming up from beneath you, and light whizzes past. Follow the roots of your tree downward, deeper and deeper, past the different strata of rocks and minerals. It becomes more and more dense; your roots become smaller, yet you find your way deeper still, until you feel your connection with the heart of Earth. You can feel the pulse of the Mother and the warmth from her fiery core. There will be something here for you, some piece of the Mother that you can take with you as you continue your journey. . . .

Bring it with you as you rise. The energy carries you upward, up through the roots and back into the tree trunk, where you can see, from the inside of the lower trunk area, the symbol of Akasha that was made when Gilgamesh attacked and scarred the tree with his axe. As you pass through that doorway, you are sucked into a vortex of night, a tunnel of darkness. The infinite twinkle of stars shines in muted splendor, as though through many layers of gauze veils. . . .

Starlight soon gives way to total emptiness as you enter the Void. Drift in this inky, velvety blackness for a timeless moment. . . .

A great eye appears. You are drawn to and pass through the pupil in the center of the eye. . . . A special gift awaits you within, something that is symbolic or that has to do with where you are in your spiritual evolution. Take up your gift, and look for the one who gave it to you. It is either the Goddess or her representative. She is there to help you learn about Akasha and how to access the records. Spend a few moments here, adjusting to the feeling of this Akashic realm and receiving information from your guide. Ask whatever questions you may have brought. . . . [*Long pause.*]

You are sent back out of the eye with new insight. Pass back through the tunnel of veiled stars and into the tree through the scar that forms the Akashic symbol. Take time to center within the trunk of the tree. Experience yourself as the total tree from within its center—whole, completely balanced and grounded, and surrounded with love. The tree transforms back into your own body, and you are in your human form again, in the presence of Thoth.

Discuss your journey with him. . . .

[*Thoth will assist you back into your ordinary consciousness.* . . .]

DOLPHIN
Communication/Atlantis

Dolphins are irresistible to most people; their happy-go-lucky antics are delightful to behold. They are extremely sensitive, playful, uninhibited mammals who have a lot to teach us about the pure joy of life.

Considerable research has been gathered toward developing linguistic communication with dolphins, for they seem to expend great effort in trying to talk to us. Many people have reported clear, telepathic communications that suggest dolphins to be intelligent, caring beings. This idea is supported by instances where dolphins have rescued people who were under attack by sharks or in the process of drowning.

Dolphins teach us that all communication consists of patterns and rhythms. As you study their communicative abilities during this journey, and in any other encounters you may have with dolphins, notice how they create the patterns and rhythms necessary for words to happen. The pauses between the sounds are also part of their language. Because of its facility as communicator, the dolphin has been called the "Hermes of the sea."

Realizing the continuity of all the actions of life is part of the dolphin's perceptions. Dolphins perceive reality as one thing melding into another; they are absolutely present within each moment. By swimming in the dolphin's world, appreciating simplicity and feeling the joy of leaping out of water into the completely alien world of air, we receive a model, a way of experiencing our lives, that gives a strong assurance of the ultimate continuance of everything that occurs.

Each time you come to visit them, dolphins will teach you more about themselves, sometimes offering an aspect of their past as dolphins or a telepathic knowledge of the cosmos. As you get to know them, you may spend more of your time as a dolphin during your journeys. Be sure to take time to resonate with your experience when you return. It is also advisable to do some extra grounding when working with Dolphin.

An aspect of Dolphin that we explore in this journey includes a primordial, feminine womb space where you will have an opportunity to gestate in a complete state of rest and receptivity. Bring no agendas with you to this place, for the nurturing you receive here is beyond delineation.

Because of the growing problem of pollution, many forms of marine life are endangered. For your gift or exchange with Dolphin, you might find a personal way of contributing in the ongoing struggle to sustain life in our oceans.

Dolphin Journey

[*Do the alchemy. . . .*]
Thoth takes you to a pristine bay of clear, blue water. There are dolphins playing in the warm water, leaping about as though they were performing just for you, waving their heads back and forth, beckoning. Enter the water to swim and play with the dolphins. They are very curious about you and not at all afraid, so you can get quite close and even stroke their sleek bodies. Pay attention to the sounds they make and their movements. They converse with one another as they frolic around you, radiating pure joy and pleasure. Take a few moments to experience this time with the dolphins. Learn how they communicate and experience dolphin play and community life. . . . [*Long pause.*]

One dolphin in particular befriends you. She invites you onto her back and carries you out into the vast expanse of ocean. Riding this sleek and graceful creature is a very sensual and slippery experience. She moves quite swiftly and purposefully. . . . [*Long pause.*]

After a lengthy swim, you come to the ancient ruins of the sunken city of Atlantis. The dolphins dive deeply into this watery past to show you around. Sand and debris cover much of the city, yet there is a sense of grandeur in the columns and architecture that can be seen. Move with the dolphins through the ruins. What you see of the buildings and monuments buried in the sand gives you a glimpse of what was once a majestic civilization.

The dolphins lead you to a hidden place with a hatch cover in the shape of a circle. A ring with carved dolphins provides a handle that must be pulled up to lift the hatch cover. It is heavy, and the dolphins help you. When the cover is opened, the dolphins wait outside and you enter through the round opening into the darkness.

It is as though you were surrounded by black, inky velvet; the atmosphere is dark, silent, almost brooding. The lack of stimulation here gives emphasis to the mysterious quality of this space. From deep within, you sense the presence of a prelingual feminine power. You have entered into the eye of the churning Cauldron in the great primordial ocean; you have returned to the womb of the Great Mother. Stay in the presence of this ancient yet formless feminine archetype to receive the gift of regeneration. . . . [*Long pause while you remain in this voidlike womb space.*]

When your time of gestation is complete, you sense contraction all around, as if the very walls of nothingness were pressing in around you. You are squeezed out of the womb, back into the water with the dolphins. You have become one of them. All of your senses are heightened, refreshed, and renewed. Feel the flowing of the water as it moves over your skin. Sound vibrations move through your body differently.

Swim as a dolphin. Enjoy the rapture of your joyous romp through the ocean with your dolphin friends. . . . [*Long pause.*]

When you have returned to the bay where Thoth waits, a dolphin nudges you and gives you a gift from the sea. . . . You can thank the dolphins in whatever way feels appropriate. The dolphins are pleased that you've made this journey and invite you to return at any time.

Consciously will yourself to step out of the water; this brings you back into human form. Take a moment to view your reflection in the clear water, so that you see your physical features. . . .

[*Thoth will help you back into your body. It is especially important to ground and center fully after working with Dolphin. If you need further assistance with grounding, looking into a mirror and seeing your human form will be helpful.*]

WERNEKE © 1991

COYOTE
Shadow Self

Coyote is the Trickster. Native Americans often call him Grandfather or Old Man Coyote, and he is greatly appreciated as a teacher. He teaches by unmasking our hidden desires. He shows us aspects of ourselves that are often surprising. His numerous feats and outrageous behavior as creator, teacher, shape-shifter, and prankster are recorded in myths and legends of many tribes and cultures all over the world.

Coyote is more than a character—he is an intriguing concept that has baffled and challenged, all who have attempted to define him. He does not always appear as an actual coyote. Some traditions know him as Hare, Crow, or Raven. In Japan, for example, the trickster is Fox, and the Egyptian equivalent is the jackal. He most definitely can be seen in Thoth.

Coyote honors the Cauldron with a journey into the "shadow self," where he brings to light that which is hidden. He helps you see what you might normally miss and lets you see it in a new light. Trickster's time is just between day and night—the crack-in-the-worlds time when magic is most potent—so this journey is best done at dusk or evening. If you cannot conveniently travel at that time, you can envision twilight. You must travel to his domain for this adventure, bounding over hillsides, through brush and trees, and maybe over high-desert terrain.

This is a hunting journey, a seeking quest. You are hunting for an experience that is a teaching for you. Coyote shows you what you need to see or confront in your own life. Of course, being Coyote, he is sure to avoid the expected. Sometimes he looks in on other people's lives. You might see how you are reflected in other people's actions. You might look in their houses, see how they act, and then recognize that those are some of the things that you do yourself. You might discover the ability to laugh at yourself or find that you have been made a fool.

The trick might be that you acquire an understanding of yourself through somebody else. You may be forced to scavenge through and eat garbage or hunt and eat a small animal. To journey with Coyote, you must do everything he does. If he runs, you run. If he jumps, you jump. Anything goes when you travel with Coyote, so be prepared and be willing to look deeply inward to uncover the hidden meaning of your lesson.

Coyote's is an open-ended journey, and it is best taken after you've had some journey experience, for when the narration stops you are on your own.

Coyote Journey

[*Do the Cauldron alchemy. . . .*]

Thoth will direct you to the domain of Coyote, and you must find him yourself. It could be woodlands or rangelands, high desert or mountains. You may see him in the underbrush, or you may have to stalk this wily critter. Coyote will be hiding somewhere in the shadows. Look into the darkest places. It will be as though you were looking into the depths of your own spirit. Meet the gaze of Coyote, for your initial connection is made through direct eye contact. . . . [*Long pause.*]

Coyote looks at you intently. His ears are perked up, alert to a range of sound that goes far beyond your normal hearing. His tongue licks at the spittle dripping from his slavering jaws. He scratches at his mangy coat, and you notice a distinctive odor that catalyzes your transformation into a lean and scruffy coyote. All your senses are heightened, especially those of smell and hearing.

You move quite swiftly in your coyote body as you follow your coyote friend. He may keep to the shadows or dart quickly across an open field or unprotected space. The more you run and the farther you go, the more your resistance dissolves so that you follow Coyote wherever he leads you. You move when he moves. When he stops, you stop. This is a journey to learn about the dark spaces, for Coyote has no fear of the dark. Allow him to take you to the appropriate experience for you at this time. . . . [*Long pause.*]

When you've had enough or feel complete, look into the eyes of Coyote again and leave a gift of some type of food for his spirit. . . . Receive whatever further message he has for you and head back to the path where Thoth waits. You will transform back into human form and recount your experience to him. . . .

[*Thoth will assist you back into ordinary consciousness. . . .*]

BLUE JAY
Masks

Masks project the multifaceted aspects of our personalities and protect us by covering those places where we feel vulnerable. We wear different masks for different occasions and situations, and we can step away from and look back at ourselves through them. They can also be used to honor different parts of ourselves, such as the warrior, the artist, the shadow, or our inner child.

Blue Jay wears many masks; he is the master of disguises. Through his ability to mimic, he becomes the sounds of other animals, yet he is still a blue jay.

Often we are deceived by the masks that other people wear. Many wear the mask of light, for example. As this world becomes more cluttered with those who say they are of the light, you must be able to see behind their masks and disguises. Blue Jay is good at unraveling the masks of others, pulling them away so that we can see their true identity and intention.

When you are out in the world and can't tell the difference between who people are and the masks that they wear, Blue Jay will help you. He can decipher the mixed messages and see through the deceptive masks of those who would change their face to suit the situation.

Once you take this journey and receive the connection to Blue Jay as ally, you will find him to be a useful friend. When you question the validity of masked beings and cannot get a clear answer, call Blue Jay and he will sit on your right hand. He will put on the appropriate mask or disclose the true face of the being you question.

As you continue to return to Blue Jay, you may get some lessons in shape-shifting from a true master.

Blue Jay Journey

[*Proceed with the alchemy. . . .*]

Thoth takes you by the hand, and together you walk out into a field. He says, "Shhh. Listen." You hear the cry of a hawk and turn and look behind, but you see no hawk. . . . Then you hear the squeak of a mouse and squat down to look in the grasses and the brush, but you can't see anything moving. . . . There are other bird noises, but you don't recognize them. . . . Now there's a squirrel sound. . . .

Thoth leads you to a fir tree and calls down a blue jay. . . . Extend your right hand; the blue jay sits on it and curls his talons around your finger, squeezing his claws until they pierce your skin. This hurts. . . . Thoth says that Blue Jay has put his mark on you. By connecting to your inner vibrations, he has become your ally.

As you look into the eye of the blue jay, you see yourself reflected, wearing the mask you display to the world. Blue Jay mimics your character. . . . You may be shown several of the masks that are your most common disguises. . . .

If you are ready and willing, Blue Jay may give you a glimpse of your true face, the one under all the masks. . . .

Blue Jay gives you a teaching about masks and how they can be used appropriately. . . . [*Long pause.*]

If there is someone in your life whose true identity you're not sure of, Blue Jay will show you his or her mask and also what's underneath. . . .

For a gift to the blue jay, you may wish to give a disguise that no longer serves you. Blue Jay is often playful and may have some fun with it. . . .

Discuss this experience with Thoth. . . .

[*Thoth will assist you back into your body. . . .*]

JACKAL
The Underworld

Native to Asia and Africa, Jackals are canines that have a folk reputation for being crafty and shrewd, as they roam the edges of the desert. They are similar to coyotes and share some of the same attributes. Their time is the darkest hour, just before the dawn, when you can hear them howl to greet the new day.

Anubis, the jackal god of Egypt, has a unique, enlightened perspective. He is guardian of the Underworld, Opener of the Way. In Egyptian theology, Anubis is the one who reads the scales at death. When a person dies, he or she is brought before the scales of Thoth, and his or her heart is weighed against the feather of Maät, the goddess who represents truth and justice.

No matter how carefully the ancient Egyptians hid and sealed their tombs, the jackal could always find ways into them. Therefore, to make the best of that adversarial condition, the Egyptians made the jackal guardian of the treasuries in the tombs. Anubis is an especially fine alchemist and is known for his mastery of the art of embalming. He also looks after miscarried and unwanted children.

With Anubis, you can safely explore the Underworld. He manifests a keenness of hearing, extreme clarity, a sharp sense of smell, and the ability to differentiate the various sources of light and darkness. His sight sees all colors, dark and light, and moves with almost the swiftness of thought. Without taking time to ponder, his awareness to act is instinctual.

Anubis is a teacher, and through his eyes, you receive education, learning, and protection. He guides people, bringing them through the darkness and back into the light. Many fear the darkness, and the knowledge that there is a guide to aid you can bring a great deal of comfort.

In the following journey, you will have an opportunity to explore weighty situations or traumatic issues in your life that may have been repressed or forgotten. In the presence of Anubis, you can shed light upon and release stuck energy that has built up around these old events or situations. Take a few moments *before* you take this journey to reflect on those issues in your life that you may be ready to deal with. It is also possible, in the presence of Anubis, to awaken memories of events that might be buried beyond your conscious memory. Relax, and give yourself permission to explore as deeply as you wish.

To meet Anubis through the Cauldron process, you will find Thoth in the darkness of the night. He directs you to the glowing eyes of the jackal that hides in the shadows. Once initiated, you can call on Anubis as guardian and protector.

Anubis Journey

[*Do the Cauldron alchemy. . . .*]
Thoth is at your left. Anubis crouches quietly in the gloom, his eyes gleaming as he looks at you. Maintain eye contact with him as you express your willingness to confront your deepest shadow issues. . . .

He greets you, acknowledges your presence, and may even sniff or lick you before he rises and takes off running. Follow him. He moves quite quickly, so you must work at keeping up. Continue following as he runs up a hill, turning around occasionally to make sure you are still with him. . . . There is a fork in the road, and Anubis goes left, running even faster. Give up wondering why. Don't even think about it.

As soon as you let go of wondering, Anubis stops and begins to dig. First he scratches the ground, then he digs straight down into the earth. He creates a hole big enough to enter into the Underworld. Inside, there is a path. You might see tree roots hanging down from above. Follow Anubis as he takes you through a series of secret tunnels, deeper and deeper into the earth. . . .

You are finally led into a chamber that is a sanctuary of initiation for you. It is very dark, so dark that pictures and colors exude from the blackness. You may now safely focus on traumatic issues and dilemmas that weigh heavily on your soul. As these issues reveal themselves to your perceptions, you gain understanding as to what you must do to achieve resolution. Options can be weighed and your intuitive side brought into balance with your pragmatic nature in dealing with the images that arise. Anubis is here for you as guardian and protector throughout this process. . . . [*Long pause.*]

When you feel complete, Anubis will guide you back to where he dug the hole. . . .

If you wish, make an offering of thanks and find your own way back along the path to Thoth. . . . Spend a moment discussing your experience with him. . . .

[*Thoth will assist you back into your body. . . .*]

PART VII

JOURNEYS FOR CELEBRATION & HONORING

There is so much about ourselves that can be learned from the Animal Kingdom, for animals display for us innate attributes we sometimes forget. We have much to honor and celebrate with these relatives regarding the richness, beauty, and pure joy of living.

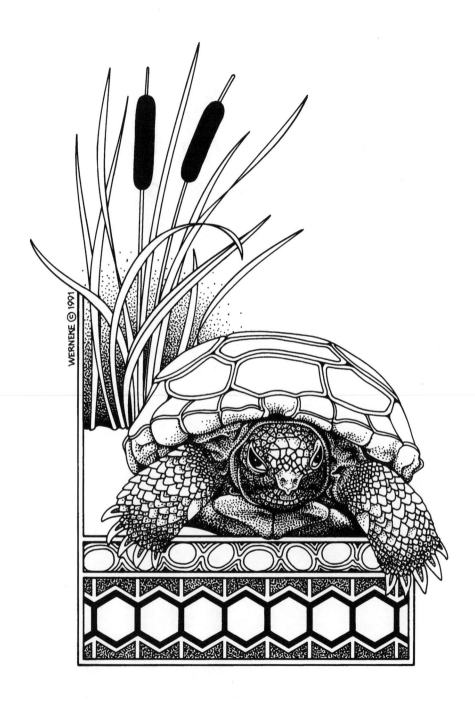

TURTLE
Service/Giving

Turtle is one of the oldest creatures on the planet. Her origins date back to the time when life first emerged from the water. Hindu mythological drawings show an image of four elephants facing out toward the four directions from the center, shouldering the world. They stand on a turtle's back.

Native Americans some call the North American continent "Turtle Island." Some South American jungle tribes believe that Turtle is the symbol of the entire planet, the "island in the sky."

Turtle represents the perpetual nature of life and its continuous regeneration, both planetary and physical. It is important to note the endurance and tolerance of Turtle; she is very forgiving, understanding, and gentle, but not naive or gullible. She has managed to maintain the same general characteristics for millennia, adapting to the earth's upheavals and evolutionary processes. She sees clearly, having a deep, earthy understanding about what's going on around her. Turtle is eternally youthful without being childlike. Comforting, maternal, and soothing, she exemplifies compassion. Yet her greatest gift is her service to future generations, through her diligent attention to the ongoing proliferation of life.

This journey came from Tawahana, the great red turtle spirit. Red represents the color of the flesh and blood of Mother Earth. There is a symbolic tie between the red tears Turtle sheds in this journey and all the unknowns, the mysteries of life, including the women's mysteries of menstrual fluids, the blood that is constructed by the body for the generation of offspring. All beings struggle to bring forth new life, and turtles exemplify the tenacity and strength required to fulfill their exhausting reproductive function. They accomplish this task without expectation of either success or failure.

The turtle breath allows us to be in touch with our entire body and its physical boundaries. It helps to expand our awareness beyond the periphery of our bodies. Before taking this journey, practice Turtle's breathing technique:

> Breathe in through your nostrils very deeply and fully, taking in as much air as you can, filling your body as though you were encased in a turtle shell. Exhale as rapidly as you can through your nose. When you breathe in this way, you feel the pressure in the front and back as though you are wearing a turtle shell.

Turtle Journey

[*Prepare by sitting very comfortably. Do five deep turtle breaths (see above). Proceed with the alchemy. . . .*]

Thoth shows you the way to the home of Turtle. You walk across the land until you come to a little lagoon with a multitude of life-forms. There are plenty of reeds and cattails, water bugs, and other insects. Notice the sunshine reflecting off the water of the lagoon. As you stare at the water, you see a movement. Coming to the surface is a very large, red turtle, who beckons you. Enter the lagoon and follow the turtle as she dives deep into the water. . . .

She comes to a stop near the bottom, and you climb onto her back. As you swim around, your form disappears and you become one with the turtle. . . . Get a sense of her body, her little webbed feet. Notice how secure you feel inside the turtle's shell, knowing you can retract yourself within it at any time.

Feel yourself as the color red, the color of Mother Earth. You feel a deep connection to the earth and understand yourself as the symbol of Turtle Island.

As Turtle, your movements are slow, deliberate, and exacting. You are perpetual and eternal, never moving in haste and never making hasty decisions. When you need air, you paddle to the surface and then swim for the shore. . . .

There is fine white sand on the beach. Walk up on the shore for a short distance, paying attention to the temperature of the sand. Find a spot that is warm, and that will stay in the sun for the longest time possible each day. Use your back legs to dig a hole that is as deep as you can reach. You are very attentive to your task and dig your hole with great compassion, care, and tenderness. Your heart chakra is wide open. When your hole is just deep enough, back into it and deposit your clutch of eggs. . . .

When you've finished laying your eggs, you, as Turtle, speak an incantation over the eggs. Gently and diligently you cover them with sand, taking great care. Your compassion for the offspring you will never know is boundless, fathomless. You fear for their safety, knowing that few of them will reach adulthood.

When they're all covered up, walk over the top of the nest, and with your left paw smooth the sand so that it doesn't look like a hole was dug there. Collect a few twigs and leaves or seaweed, and scatter them on top for camouflage.

When you're done, walk slowly across the beach to the water. Red tears roll down from your eyes, leaving red drops in the sand.

Go back into the water, dive deeply, and stop to rest on the bottom. Your body separates from Turtle. Climb off her back and swim around to face her and look deeply into her eyes for a long, long time. She may give you a message that is a special teaching for you at this time. . . . [*Long pause.*]

You may wish to make an appropriate offering. . . .

When your communication with Turtle is complete, she will swim along with you, guiding you down the lagoon to the point where you first entered the water. Follow the path to where Thoth waits.

Spend a few moments with him. . . .

[*Thoth will assist you back into your body.* . . .]

BEAVER
Responsibility/Industriousness

Beaver was always an important food source for native peoples throughout the North American continent, but after the white man came, trapping beaver for fur became central to the economy of many tribes. Subarctic Native Americans who left their nomadic ways to settle in permanent villages and became traders also became dependent on European trade goods. Overtrapping, partially due to a beaver-hat fad, made beavers scarce and, in some places, virtually extinct by the early nineteenth century, leaving these unlucky traders destitute. Disease and alcoholism left them as endangered as the beaver they had hunted.

Beavers have played a major role in water and land management throughout North America for hundreds of years, thinning the forests and creating dams. Now, however, they are often considered pests and a detriment to the forest.

In the Cauldron, the journey with Beaver is intended to give assistance in bearing the responsibilities of daily life creatively. He can help us be more productive and industrious in our activities. Beaver does what needs to be done without wasting energy through procrastination. He provides impetus for creativity in the most menial of tasks and uses his instincts to get his task completed in the most efficient manner, for he is very industrious and loves to work.

Beavers teach us about harmonious teamwork, for in the development of their building projects all input is equal, and every action fulfills a necessary function; everyone in a beaver community is an artist or designer. Beaver epitomizes the adage "Before enlightenment, chop wood and carry water; after enlightenment, chop wood and carry water."

Beaver Journey

[Do the Cauldron alchemy. . . .]

Standing next to Thoth is a beaver. The beaver is little, standing on his haunches, balancing on his flat, broad tail. He chews voraciously. "Come follow me," he beckons. The beaver drops to his feet and walks to Thoth's right, into a woodsy area where young maples have been felled. The fallen trees are not very big around. You can see the teeth marks where they have been chewed.

Beaver climbs up onto your shoulders, rests his head on your head, and puts his little, cold feet over your eyes. He begins to feel like a hood, and then a coat, and now you feel like you have your own beaver tail. You're sharing his body; his thoughts enter your head. Sit back on your haunches and feel the balance of your tail. It feels secure. It's not heavy but, rather, lightweight.

Drop down to all fours and walk toward the pond. Look at the trees from the perspective of Beaver. There is one that is perfect for the dam that he is building. Experience what it is like to chew the wood with your large, sharp teeth. When the tree is down, clear the branches and select the particular piece of wood you need to take out to the dam at this time. Pick it up and enter the water.

Beaver's body feels light and buoyant in the water, as does the piece of wood; there's no effort involved in carrying it. You understand that responsibility is like the wood: if you see its buoyancy, it is not a burden.

Your instincts tell you the right spot to place the wood in the dam. Always pay attention to these instincts. Practice going to and from the pond to the shore, getting wood and putting it in the dam. Each time you select a piece of a different size, and each time you are able to find a place where it belongs—where it fits perfectly. Do this at least three times. . . . *[Long pause.]*

When you finish, it's time to go underneath the dam and into Beaver's den. The doorway is underwater, but the inside is above water, almost beehive shaped. Once inside, you are a part of the community. There are several adults and some young beavers sharing the food and the warmth. During your communication with these beavers, you are given a teaching about responsibility in your own life. . . . *[Pause.]*

When you feel complete with this experience, think of Thoth. As your light body rises out of Beaver's head, thank him for sharing his world with you. He thanks you for coming. An appropriate gift for Beaver is your willingness to experience his world so he could share what he has to share—his unique perspective on life.

Discuss your experience with Thoth. . . .

[*Thoth will assist you back into your ordinary consciousness. . . .*]

WERNEKE © 1991

RAVEN

Reclaiming Childhood

Raven stories are predominant in Native American mythology of the American Northwest, and they are also strong in Celtic, Chinese, and Japanese cultures. Raven is a trickster who outwits by outthinking; he is very manipulative and vocal and usually gets other people to do his work for him. He is often seen as a glutton with a tendency to gorge until he becomes sick. In many Native American stories, Raven appears as a cohort of Coyote in misadventures and, like Coyote, is often the butt of his own jokes. Ravens are excellent pickpockets; they are attracted to shiny things, and you will find such objects woven into their nests.

In many traditions, Raven is a symbol for sorcery and magic. The European sorcerer would take the form of Raven, as would the shape-shifters of Japan. He depicts the black powers of the night, the shadow of the black bird with wings spread full. Raven is a messenger from the dark side. He can fly into the void and back, carrying messages and healings between the worlds. Seeing him can be an omen of impending change.

Raven also forewarns of danger. He awakens the forest to any intruders, alerting all the animals to those who are about and what they're up to, especially people. Native Americans of the Northwest used to mimic the calls of Raven to warn each other when enemies were close.

As an ally, Raven is especially beneficial for those who have had difficult childhoods, for he is able to get into the dark places where fear and tension lurk, break them down, and help get rid of them. He can find the hidden places of physical and emotional abuse and lighten things up to prepare the way for healing. Raven helps people reclaim the joy that was once theirs or that they missed.

Raven is also very spontaneous and has the childlike ability to go after what he wants in a very direct way, whether it is a glittering jewel or a safety pin. "Shoulds" and "don'ts" are not in his conditioning. He helps recapture that special childlike frame of mind. For those of you who have managed to retain the positive qualities of your childhood, this journey gives you an opportunity to celebrate. Let yourself get into the mischievous nature of Raven and have fun with this one!

Journey Preparation

This journey is somewhat complex, but it is well worth the effort. Preparation is required. Visualize four aspects of your childhood that were important to you. Whether or not you had these things is not as significant as that you wanted them. Choose carefully those things of most value.

Transform each of these aspects into four trinkets or toys, objects to symbolize your attachment to them. For example, if you wanted to be lucky, you might pick a rabbit's foot to symbolize that quality. Or if you wanted to excel in athletic competition, you could choose a blue ribbon or a trophy. Maybe you wanted to be the head of your class. A "straight A" report card would be a good symbol for that.

Next, take the four trinkets and prominently place them in your life, where you would like them to be. You might put the blue ribbon on the wall and the rabbit's foot on your night stand. You can do this part with your imagination in your own meditation or physically, if that seems appropriate.

Determine in advance where your hiding place, the stash where you will hide the booty, will be located.

Raven Journey

[When everything is in place in your mind—or physically, if you chose to do it that way—go through the Cauldron alchemy. . . .]
Thoth will pass you through a doorway into the dark realm of Raven. As you enter, your arms become wings and you have a sense of yourself

as dark, black, and nervous. You feel strangely playful and extremely mischievous—so mischievous that you dance around incessantly when you're not flying. You can't sit still.

Fly to where the symbols of your achievements are displayed. Feel yourself become more and more agitated as you observe these treasures, flaunted right out in the open for everyone to see. You want them all to yourself, hidden somewhere where no one else can have them. They are so precious that you don't even want anyone to know you're going to retrieve them. Wait till you're sure no one is looking. . . . [Pause.]

Now dash out and get one of the valued trinkets, and as soon as you retrieve it, fly to your most secret of places in today's reality, the hiding place you've selected, and stash your trinket. . . .

Do not leave your cache until you are sure that no one will see you. Now go and retrieve the other three trinkets, one at a time, until all of the representations are hidden in your secret place. . . . [Long pause.]

When you have brought all four cherished trinkets to your secret place, display them ornamentally and dance and sing with delight. This dance is your thank-you for the journey. You can actually dance, or you can imagine yourself dancing in your mind. . . .

Dance until you're danced out, and then fly back to Thoth. . . . Recount your experience to him. . . .

[Thoth will help you back. . . .]

FIELD MOUSE
Humility

Small and humble, the field mouse has many things to teach humans. Field mice have a connection to the earth that is so different from that of humans that is difficult for us to comprehend. A large part of their world exists in the space created by our footprints as we walk through a field. When you take this journey, you get to experience and appreciate what it's like to be small.

Field Mouse is a tiny creature, hunted by owls and many other predators. Constantly the prey of large forces beyond his control, he has an appreciation of the earth and recognizes his smallness next to these greater beings that can swoop down and pluck him from life. Field Mouse lives gratefully on the earth, knowing that at any time his life can come to a sudden end.

If it is possible, this journey is best taken in the woods, a field, or perhaps a park—a large wilderness park would be best, but your backyard will do. For those who cannot be outside, get a tape or record of bird songs or nature sounds and perhaps a picture of a field—maybe even a pot of dirt to put your hands in. The combination of the picture, the sounds, the feel of the dirt, and your imagination will be sufficient.

If you undertake this journey outdoors, you will do best to actually lie on the ground. If you are afraid of insects, remember that they are more frightened of you, for you are capable of doing much more harm to them than they are to you. If you wish, bring a magnifying glass, but be careful not to kill a being that you may think is insignificant with the focused heat of the sun.

It is important for humans to realize the sacredness of simplicity. We tend to be demanding, always wanting the most and highest for ourselves, even on a spiritual level, and forcing our will onto our environment. Field mice have a richness in their lives that comes from living in harmony with the elements. Theirs is a way of gentleness, of bending; they find strength through acceptance. Field mice use the few materials around them to make very simple homes, and yet they experience a love of the earth on levels that our complicated lives seldom allow.

This is a journey of few words.

Field Mouse Journey

[*Bring lots of patience and quiet with you. Lie on your belly in a field of grass. Do not prop your head up above the grass. When your chin is resting on the ground and the grass is at eye level, do the Cauldron alchemy and enter the world of Field Mouse. . . .*]

There is an environment at this level that is as complete and unique as yours. Notice the insects, the teeming life that lives in the soil. When you live so very close to the skin of the Mother, you are very aware of how dependent we are on her being and on her sharing.

Spread your arms out to your sides as if to embrace the earth. Rest your chin on the soil, and stay for as long as your body will allow you. Imagine yourself as a mouse living in this area. You will feel yourself as quite small, and your nose might twitch to catch the fragrance of the surroundings. . . .

Extend your consciousness in all directions. Feel yourself a part of this realm. If you truly humble yourself and observe this domain with keen focus, while feeling with your heart, you will develop an awareness and connection that will greatly benefit your being. You will never again view the earth the same way as before.

As you lie with arms spread, belly down in the field or in the woods—even in your backyard—open your heart and feel the life of the planet that's beneath your body. This is indeed a miracle in itself. Just let yourself feel the joy of being able to hug the earth, to smell the grass, to feel the air and the sun. This simple experience should be enough to bring you happiness and great joy.

[*Thoth will assist you back into your body. . . .*]

WERNEKE © 1991

PEACOCK
Magic/Graciousness/Generosity

Peacock is a somewhat controversial totem. Some cultures consider peacock feathers to be bad luck, especially for gambling, while others recognize in the exquisite feathers the all-seeing eye, representing great fortune and power. Peacock feathers can be used to ward off evil spirits, according to some Hindus and Moslems. Peacock is the national bird of India, and the throne of Persia was called the "Peacock Throne."

Peacock has ancient knowledge about magic and can work energy to create anything he desires. Because his wants are few, he makes the best of his time here on Earth, fabricating a gorgeous, sumptuous setting in which to present himself. He is facile with this environment and likes what he has created.

Peacock is quite playful—a hedonist, in fact—but this doesn't bother him. There is no self-criticism or denial here. He encompasses, in a warm, openhanded way, the ability to relish and envelop life. He would laugh at our judgments, for he enjoys himself without being kept from Spirit.

A large and graceful bird, Peacock realizes he lives in a body on the earth plane and needs to enjoy his abilities to manifest hedonistic pleasures. He has the ability to take it all lightly and with humor. He is the perfect king, loving and regal. Although he has a beautiful form, he is not attached to it—being in a body is the same as being in a mask. Once we have mastered the ability to put masks on and take them off at will, we can come into our bodies with a new sense of freedom to play.

Peacock has a lot to teach about treating things with humor, the kind of humor that keeps us from abusing power. It's a gift to be able to pull things out of the air. Like all gifts, it must be approached with gratitude and joy. There is great generosity about this being.

For some, this journey is simply about being in the presence of Peacock, finding rapport with that awesome ability to manifest without becoming attached or falsely prideful. Real pride comes from a deep place of generosity. Peacock can mirror your own generosity and show you how to accept gifts and not use them to manipulate others. There is majesty in Peacock that can appear as pompousness, depending on the perspective of the visitor. If you come with admiration and envy, you will learn another set of lessons, for he will mirror envy and pride.

This experience is also about magnificence. Allow yourself the full experience of Peacock's splendor in order to understand his ability to manifest while being surrounded by beautiful, seductive gorgeousness!

Peacock Journey

[*Do the alchemy. . . .*]

As you come out of the alchemy and into the presence of Thoth, your attention is drawn to a thrumming sensation, a vibration, which must be experienced to attain resonance with Peacock; it feels somewhat like a drumming in your ears. By resonating to this vibration, you break through barriers of time and space to tune into frequencies where Peacock's manifesting capabilities can occur. The thrumming continues and will be more or less apparent throughout the entire journey.

Thoth points the way, and you come to a spacious green lawn with a pagoda in the distance. You can feel from the air that you are at a high altitude. Pine trees, thin crackly air, and a crisp blue sky highlight this scene. The pagoda has a gold dome, and its inside is reminiscent of a four-poster bed with a canopy. Gold balls crown the posts, and steps on either side facilitate accessibility. Peacocks are wandering about on the lawn.

As you move closer to the pagoda, you see piles of pillows heavily embroidered with golden thread. There are rich carpets of the finest Persian silk on the ground, bowls with water and incense, and offerings of grain and flowers. In the middle of the pillows, enthroned in this oblong temple, sits a splendid peacock.

Walk in closer. As you climb the steps, your inclination might be to bow to this noble bird. He tells you to come and sit at his side. You sit next to him and admire his feathers, his long silken neck, and the colorful crest at the top of his head. You can't see his talons, as they are tucked under him. This peacock is quite comfortable with his beauty, royalty, and pride, and he is quite happy to have you there to share the surrounding splendor of his domain. He wants to enfold you in that feeling so that you, too, can experience this elegance, comfort, and royal bearing.

Notice the inclusive feeling here; Peacock doesn't have to shut people out. He offers you some things to eat: dried apricots, coconut, and seeds. No one brought them—they simply appeared.

Follow the gaze of Peacock as he surveys his well-tended domain. The sumptuous green blanket of lawn stretches in every direction, replete with beauty, symmetry, and grace. It feels ancient, as though it had been here for a very long time.

Peacock is capable of performing magic and can pull things out of the air. He hands you a gift that he pulls out of thin air and a teaching that is appropriate to your visit at this time. . . . [*Long pause.*]

This peacock gets pleasure from giving, and a thank-you is his greatest reward. You need not admire him—to share with him is sufficient. When your time is complete, leave the pagoda and walk down the lawn, where you will meet Thoth. Share this experience with him. . . .

[*Thoth will assist you back. . . .*]

WERNEKE © 1991

WHITE BUFFALO
Reverence/Ancestors

Buffalo were vital to the Plains Indians. They provided food, clothing, shelter, and tools. White buffalo were extremely unusual, and to see one was considered a rare and auspicious omen, a highly regarded gift from Spirit. When the buffalo were slaughtered, these Native Americans suffered the loss of their way of life.

White Buffalo Woman is revered in North America, especially by the Plains Indians, as the one who brought the Sacred Pipe to the people. According to legend, it was a particularly severe winter when two scouts headed out in search of food for the people of a band of Lakota Sioux. A woman approached them out in the wilderness, and one of the men looked upon her with lust, even over the objections of the other scout, who recognized her as *wacan*, which means "sacred" or "holy." When the first man spoke of his intentions to his friend, the woman invited him to step forward, and as he did he and the woman were enveloped in a cloud of dust or smoke. When the air cleared, at the woman's feet was a pile of bones with snakes eating them. She addressed the remaining scout and told him to go back to his village and prepare for her coming, as she would be there the next day and had gifts for the people. The villagers were to prepare a large tepee in a sacred manner.

The next day, the woman arrived and was welcomed by the tribespeople. She carried with her the bundle within which was the original Sacred Pipe. She told the people that if they continued to smoke the pipe in accordance with her instructions and followed the ceremonies she taught them during her stay, they would grow in strength and prosper. If not, they would become weak and wither away.

The pipe was given to them as a means to reach Great Spirit and to pray; it functions among other things as an intermediary. When her stay was complete and she had imparted the gifts and teachings to the people, the woman left the circle, and as she walked out of the village, she turned into a white buffalo calf. Hence, the original pipe is called the White Buffalo Calf Pipe, and the woman is known as White Buffalo Woman. This relic remains a central icon of the Lakota and other tribes of the Sioux nation, and is still held safe and sacred in South Dakota today.

White Buffalo Woman is an important deity for anyone searching for a path of harmony in the Great Mystery. She gives teachings about reverence and sacredness. She also imparts a sense of feminine strength, the strength of the Mother. The corresponding goddess in Egypt would be Hathor, the all-nurturing Cow, the Mother Goddess who provides abundance for the people. In India, the cow is held sacred as well.

The following journey came into the Cauldron in a magical way, as a direct result of a giveaway of the teachings. The giveaway seems to be the essence of this wonderful and powerful being; giveaways come from the heart. The ritual of the giveaway has long been practiced by many tribes to honor or give thanks. It can be the giveaway of anything or everything. It can be a piece of meat, a symbol, or a great teaching that can change one's path in life. Under certain circumstances a person would be required to give away all that he or she owned.

White Buffalo Woman can work with you on your issues around manifestation, helping you get past blocks and barriers that keep you from the abundance and joy she represents. You can also ask her about family or community. She may appear as either a buffalo or a woman, or both. I hold this journey in great value and share it with you in the spirit of the giveaway.

This journey is enhanced by shamanic drumming. If you have a drum or a tape of shamanic drumming, a steady rhythm would be an appropriate background addition.

White Buffalo Journey

[Do the Cauldron alchemy. . . .]

Thoth points to a plain. The wind is blowing from the north, and as far as you can see, grasses are rippling in the breeze. As you become familiar with the plain and its expansive vibration, you are aware of buffalo all around you. You are in the midst of a herd, with some wandering about, some grazing. Tune in to the buffalo and begin to take on resonance with their essential spirit, until you feel yourself change into one of them. You feel his or her massive head in front of your own. As you feel yourself become a buffalo, you stomp your foot and flick your tail. . . .

Flare your nostrils and take five buffalo breaths, in and out through your nose with great force, preparing for the charge. On the final exhale, you charge out across the great plain, pounding the earth with your hooves, thundering across the great expanse of space. . . .

You come to a place where there are boulders, but you can't see what's on the other side. As you leap over the rocks, the ground vanishes—you have fallen over the steep cliff! You lose yourself, falling, as though your whole reality has been yanked from under you. Feel the horror of falling—it is as though your will is being pulled away. You fall to the death of your old way, crash landing on the generations of the bones of your ancestors at the bottom of the cliffs. . . . There is a teaching here for you from your ancestors. . . . [*Long pause.*]

When you stand up, the bones are gone, the cliffs are gone, and you are at peace. Buffalo are all around you. There is a sense of both eternity and community here. Notice how it feels to be a part of, and move about with, the other buffalo. There is a sense of one-mindedness. It is as though this alternate reality is superimposed upon the great plains. As your focus clarifies, you become aware of the presence of great power, gentleness, and strength as White Buffalo approaches. You may feel a sense of reverence and awe. Greet her with respect and receive the message or gift she brings to you. It may be a great teaching or a living symbol. . . . [*Long pause.*]

In the spirit of the giveaway, make an offering to White Buffalo. . . .

When your time with White Buffalo is complete, walk away from her and pass through the veil that separated you from the great plain, where you will again take your human form. Thoth will be there to spend a moment sharing this experience. . . .

[*Thoth will assist you back into your body through your crown. Be sure to ground and center in your body.* . . .]

PART VIII

JOURNEYS FOR LIBERATION

This section of Power Animal Meditations *is devoted to clearing the way for liberation from the constraints of limited thoughts and beliefs. Old patterns are relinquished, making way for new, expanded views that generate a sense of greater connection with the Whole of Creation.*

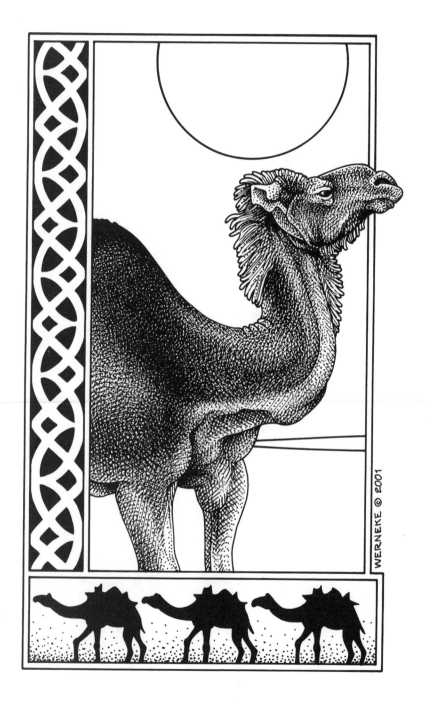

WERNEKE © 2001

CAMEL
Finding Your Way/Endurance/
Developing Intuition

The one-humped Arabian camel, found in many parts of western Asia and northern Africa, is widely honored for its unique powers of endurance. The camel is renowned for its ability to carry heavy burdens on long treks across the harsh desert, with little need for food or water. The Bedouins call camels *ata Allah,* "God's gift," out of gratitude for the multitude of essential services they offer. In addition to transportation, camels provide milk, meat, and hides; wool for clothing, rope, and paintbrushes; and even shade from the hot sun. Their capacity for retaining fluids is so efficient that when their dung is excreted, it is dry enough to be burned for fuel. Their tolerance for fluctuating body temperatures, extraordinary capacity for water retention, and slow absorption of water all contribute to their ability to go for days without anything to drink.

Camels are always prepared, for at any moment they may be asked to journey for days with little or no refreshment. Their humps are used to store not water but fat, which can be converted into energy when food is scarce. Although reputed to be ill tempered and obstinate, camels are actually patient and intelligent. They tend to be unpredictable rather than unpleasant.

When everything looks most bleak, Camel comes to help those who are lost and in despair. He strengthens your power to endure and helps you learn to trust your own intuition for guidance. Every time you take this journey with Camel, you add to your base of knowledge and increase your intuitive capabilities. Finally you will possess an inner knowledge of the entire desert, the whole landscape of your life—you can even see to the other side. When you know where you are, how to find your way at each and every moment, you need never fear the unknown or the winds of change. You can plot a true course, no matter how the wind and shifting sands may obscure your outer vision.

Camel Journey

[*Do the Cauldron alchemy.* . . .]

When you come into the presence of Thoth, you find yourself in the midst of a vast desert. As you look around, you see a landscape of sandy, barren, hills stretching in every direction. You realize that you have no idea where you are or how you could possibly find your way out of this desolate place. There are no landmarks here, for the sand dunes move ceaselessly. The wind wails and the sand blows so that it creates a cloud of dust that obscures your vision, though you are able to make out rippling shapes and shifting patterns on the rolling hills. . . . Being lost reminds you of the shifting and changing events in your everyday life, which have left you feeling disoriented. You're not sure how to integrate all the changes. Allow these issues to come into focus. . . . [*Pause.*]

Make your way up to the top of the highest dune and look down the other side, where there is a small gully protected from the wind. There, resting in the gully, you see a camel. He is lying down, at his ease, and he eyes you as you come toward him. As you approach this camel, open your heart honestly and fully, and make eye contact with him. Acknowledge that you may be lost and ask him to help you to find your way. . . . [*Pause.*]

Climb onto the camel's back and settle yourself in the wide saddle—lean forward, then back as the camel lurches and rises to stand. He strides off across the desert at a comfortable, easy, steady gait. You feel yourself being pushed forward and backward, which rocks your third chakra, the solar plexus area between your heart and belly that rules your personal will and power. As you become accustomed to the rhythm, it becomes second nature and you develop a sense of oneness with the camel. . . . As you become more and more comfortable, its movement begins to make intuitive sense and you find yourself starting to share consciousness with your new camel friend. . . . [*Pause.*]

Begin to notice how the camel gets his bearings in this vast desert. Subtleties such as the quality of light and angle of the sun, the direction and taste of the wind, and the length and direction of the shadows start to take on meaning. Although there are no stationary landmarks, it is as though a map has been laid over the entire landscape, even beyond the obscured horizons. You begin to recognize roughly where you are in relationship to the oases, mountains, and towns at the edges of the desert. You have a definite sense of knowing where water is—you can feel its energy under the ground and can tell where that energy is stronger and where it is weaker. . . . You realize that you are not controlling this camel; rather, you are merging memories and becoming of one mind, so that this totally unknown desert suddenly becomes familiar. . . . [*Long pause.*]

You are no longer floundering, and you are filled with the realization that you can never be lost again, for you will always have the ability to determine exactly where you are in relation to all the support and nourishment you require. . . . You have become totally aware of the moisture content of your body and how to balance that awareness with the knowledge of how many days you are from any place where you can replenish your moisture.

Your awareness of your real-life situation increases, and you are able to begin reassessing your priorities. What you may have viewed as crucially important, even as distressing or insurmountable, when you began this journey now attains a place of less concern as you establish which of your goals are within reach and which are not. . . . [*Pause.*]

The wind has dropped to a light breeze. You feel calm as you plod onward confidently and unerringly to where you know you must go. You can feel your destination with your whole body. . . . Knowing where you are going puts everything into a different context. . . . Your priorities are coming into better focus. . . . As you gain a sense of clarity about what is most important and where you need to get to in your life, you are able to move steadily in the right direction. . . . [*Pause.*]

Thoth appears. The camel stops and drops down to his knees to allow you to step off his back. . . . As a gift for your camel, you may wish to offer an apple and perhaps a red and gold tassel for his bridle.

Remember, you should always show great kindness to your camel. . . .
Relate your experience to Thoth, who has been following your journey
and has come to meet you at its conclusion. . . .

[*Thoth will assist you back into your physical body and ordinary reality.
Ground and center before opening your eyes. . . .*]

PELICAN

Nurturing and Protecting Your Inner Child

Pelican is one of the few creatures that have lived on Earth almost unchanged since prehistoric times. In mystical traditions, Pelican has attained almost mythical status as a religious icon. She is legendary in Christianity as one who, like Christ, sacrifices her own blood for the sake of her children. In his entry about Pelican in *A Dictionary of Symbols,* J. E. Cirlot says, "An aquatic bird, which, as legend has it, loved its young so dearly that it nourished them with its own blood, pecking open its breast to this end. It is one of the best-known allegories of Christ. . . ." In alchemy, Pelican is the alembic, the womb or receptacle in which life is transformed, and also represents the stage called *mortificatio,* when one's outer shell is broken open to reveal the true inner being.

Pelican protects her young with a ruthless determination. She knows that no one will protect them except for her, so she is fierce, staunch, and uncompromising. It is her mission to protect youth and she is driven by purely instinctual, maternal, and primal knowing. Even when everything is perfect, she must go one step further.

This journey with Pelican features her role as protector of the inner child. This is an important role because a healthy, secure, fully integrated inner child is the dynamo that keeps each of us spinning in balance. Pelican helps us hold that aspect of ourselves in a nurturing and supportive way, which allows our inner child to be heard and accepted. As mature adults, or even older children, we need to come forth to protect our inner child, because no one else will do that for us. Doing so helps us integrate our beings so that there won't be separation between the child and the woman or man it has become. There is a point of integration where we come into unity, into wholeness. It is important when you journey with Pelican to remember that she is an aspect of yourself, a more evolved aspect looking back on a less evolved one and nurturing it along.

Pelican Journey

[*Do the alchemy. . . .*]

Thoth meets you when you come out of the alchemy and points the way to a beach, where you find yourself on fine, white sand surrounded by sun-bleached driftwood and occasional shells. This beach is a place of innocence—of newness and clarity. Everything is clean. The sun is bright; the air is warm and clear and it smells fresh like the sea. It is easy to return to an age of carefree youth, to a time of safety and innocence. The waves are gentle, and you find yourself walking and jumping, running, and feeling happy.

There are cliffs that run parallel to the shore, and you begin to climb up the sides of them. Your small child body clambers over rocks, and you sense that something guides you, even though the way is arduous. You grab onto rocks to help pull yourself up. It's easy to find handholds and toeholds to assist you in your climb, and you continue even when the way seems so difficult that you wonder if you can make it.

You are instinctively drawn toward a particular spot. From above comes the sharp cry of the pelican. You can hear her as you climb, and you can feel the ocean spraying your face as the waves, which were so gentle, grow more violent below. Finally you arrive at the top, where the pelican nest is, and there is a great, beautiful mother pelican waiting for you. She spreads her wings in welcome, and when she gathers you into them, you feel as if you are her child. She touches you on your forehead with her beak and you know that it is okay to rest now—you are safe. Take a moment to fully realize this feeling of safety with all of your senses. . . . [*Pause.*]

Close your eyes and go more deeply inside. Mother Pelican takes her grand bill and pierces her breast, drawing her sacred blood to feed you. . . . You are infused with all the protection and vigilance you will ever need. From now on, you can carry it with you, and you will always know in your heart that you are safe. . . . As Pelican's blood nourishes you, you feel your inner child—the child who you have become on this journey—begin to integrate with the grown-up who you are in everyday reality. . . . See your inner child standing vulnerable and alone; then let your awareness expand to include your adult body. Feel yourself as an adult with your inner child held safely within. . . . [*Pause.*]

When you feel whole and complete unto yourself, receive the transmissions of Pelican's ancient wisdom. . . . [*Long pause.*] Notice that you feel as though your heart is growing wings. You can gather yourself into your own giant wings, wrapping them around you when you need protection.

Pelican picks you up and carries you in the expandable pouch under her bill. She flies down from the top of the cliff and soars out over the sea, which has become calm again. She dips you in the cool, salty water, then gently places you on the beach where you began your journey. . . . She leaves you on the sand, then flies back to her nest, her broad wings flapping. She lets out a great cry. The vibration of her cry solidifies the teaching in your body and your soul. You know that all you have to do is listen for that frequency, remember or create that sound, and it will bring her back at any time.

Your gift to Pelican is your commitment to protect the children, and lest you forget, when you hear her cry, you will remember. Protection of the children is the hope and protection of the future. We must create a safe future for our children and for the planet.

Thoth appears. Share your experiences with him. . . .

[*Thoth will assist you back into your body. . . . Be sure to ground and center. . . .*]

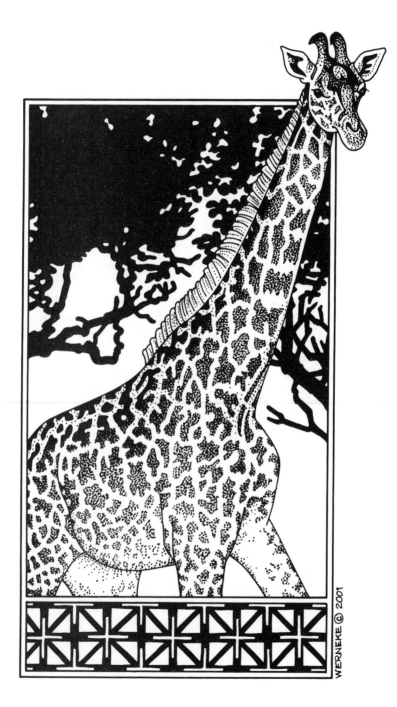

WERNEKE © 2001

GIRAFFE
Seeing from the Heart

Giraffe is a gentle creature who sees life from a unique perspective. The tallest of the animals, she is afforded a view from an exceptional height, while her broad stance maintains her strong connection to the earth. Giraffe has a huge heart, and with all her being, she perceives heart's dimension, seeing and feeling the heart connections between herself and the entire web of life. In leading you on this journey, she gives you an opportunity to ask for help and cooperation. She knows that there are only loving relationships in the realm of the heart, relationships in which each being nurtures the flame of every other being.

Although related to the dimension of words and actions, the dimension of the heart is completely independent. Giraffe reminds us to make regular trips to the heart dimension to honor and affirm this network of loving light. The more we practice viewing our everyday communications and interactions within the context of this loving web, the more accessible and clearly manifest the web becomes.

Giraffe also bestows this gift: the knowledge that your heart is a place in which only truth can reside. Whenever you speak to another being, a simultaneous conversation takes place in the heart dimension. It is a conversation of truth, and this, from the perspective of your soul, is what truly matters.

Giraffe Journey

[*Do the alchemy. . . .*]
Once in the presence of Thoth, return your focus to your heart flame and direct love so that it will expand and brighten and grow. . . . [*Pause.*]

In the light of your heart flame, you find yourself in the vast, open grasslands of Africa, known as the veldt. This spacious landscape is dotted with tall trees that have wide, spreading crowns. Walk up to one of the trees and listen to the wind playing gently in its leaves and rippling through the grass.

Place your hands on the tree's bark and feel its hard, solidly rooted trunk. . . . Look up into its canopy of leaves. This tree would be easy to climb, so you grasp a stout branch and pull yourself up. Then, reaching hand over hand, you climb high into the crown.

When you find a secure perch, look out across the veldt from this new perspective. All your senses have heightened, and you notice a rustling noise beside you. Turn your head and find yourself looking into the gentle eyes of Giraffe.

While you look into her eyes, let your attention be drawn to your heart. The heart connection you make with this giraffe invites your own heart to expand. Notice how it feels when you allow your heart to open further. . . . [*Pause.*] In the light of your expanded heart, you begin to see the faces of those that you feel closest to. Feel your connections to these beings. Notice as filaments of golden light take shape, linking this gathering of kindred spirits to one another and creating a small network, a family, a clan.

The mutual acceptance that exists within this family strengthens your connections within this web. For every part of you that feels unloved, there is a being in this network who loves that part of you. You begin to recognize wholeness within this loving structure. . . . Take a few moments to notice some specific relationships; acknowledge them, and give thanks. . . . This is an opportunity for one heart to speak to another. . . . [*Long pause.*]

Now allow your vision of the network to expand, and you will perceive more golden filaments connecting to more loving hearts, spreading and growing until the filaments of light form a glowing, jeweled network around the entire globe. . . . This luminous web is nearly invisible, so take a moment to acknowledge and strengthen it. . . . [*Pause.*]

For each sharing of the light given, a sharing is returned—even if words and actions do not seem to reflect it—because now we are in the dimension of the heart. . . . Take a few moments for deeper reflection from this loving space. Allow yourself to fully bask in the wholeness, and spend as much time here as you like. . . . [*Long pause.*]

When you feel complete, thank Giraffe for sharing her special perspective. . . . Now, as you look out over the veldt, you can see how each animal and plant in the wide, open range exists in loving relationship with all the others.

Climb back down from the tree and return to Earth. Ground and center yourself.

Remember Giraffe's gentleness and make that a part of yourself. No matter how correct or incorrect you may think yourself or another to be, gentleness and kindness are always appropriate. This is the gift of the heart.

The memory of Giraffe's loving gaze will always be in your heart to remind you that you need never be afraid to look into the eyes of others, where you will always see the truth.

[*Thoth will help you back into your physical body. . . .*]

Horned Lizard
Armoring/Conscious Evolution

Horned Lizard, who is sometimes referred to as Horny Toad, is an endangered species that resides mostly in Texas. He is very shy, and his lessons speak to issues of loneliness, alienation, and poor self-image. Because he is by nature solitary, you will need to seek him out and engage him in the journey. Horned Lizard is related to chameleons, although he does not have as much in his surroundings to hide behind. In the way that chameleons change color according to their surroundings, this lizard will change his picture of himself as you journey together. In the course of this joint venture, both of you will learn a good deal about yourselves and each other.

During your time together, Horned Lizard shares his evolutionary process with you, explaining how he grew his spines to ensure his survival. In the safety of the trust that develops between you, you begin to recognize who you are beneath your own protective shields and to explore your own lifelong process of creating self-protection.

When you share your stories with Horned Lizard, your body and soul will remember, at a cellular level, that early time before you felt the need for self-protection, for the invisible armor that shields you. This is a wonderful opportunity for you to participate in your own evolution. Horned Lizard provides you with a safe space where you can step out of the protective armor you have created in the same way that a lizard sheds its skin, even if only temporarily. That is his gift to you. You needn't feel pressured to reveal yourself—let go of your protective armor only when you are ready.

Horned Lizard will receive whatever protection you release and will add it to his own DNA. Even if you can contribute just one cell, you will affect the evolution of his entire species. As a human being, you have passed through the reptilian stage, whereas he has never been a human. Our needs are very different from his. We use our minds to create psychological protection in a way that the reptilian brain cannot fathom. Yet Horned Lizard can transform your cerebral need for protection into a physical protection for himself and his species, so that his offspring will grow sharper spines or faster legs than their predecessors had.

Whatever armor you reclaim or decide to keep at the end of the journey is entirely up to you. But in the safe space provided by Horned Lizard, you can revisit the choices of your childhood informed by the perspective of your adult wisdom. From your new perspective, you will be free to make different choices about who you are and what serves you well in the present. Horned Lizard helps you step out from behind your protective screen to recognize the perfection of who you are right now.

Horned Lizard Journey

[*Do the alchemy. . . .*]

You meet Thoth in a crowded place, such as a train station or mall or airport. As you walk together, you feel prickly spines projecting from your body in all directions. Passing through the crowd of people, you notice that everybody gives you plenty of room, as though your prickly armor is a physical part of your body that keeps others at bay.

As you continue walking, you become aware that every other person in this crowded place is wearing an armored shield as well. You can see how the true nature of each person is covered and hidden in this way. As you pass people who have been wounded by unhappy childhoods, you are aware of their loneliness, seeing it in the way they carry themselves. A deeply injured person carries excess body weight, visible here as spines grown to keep away marauding relatives, and everyone else as well. Another person appears as a frightened child whose adult body, covered in thick, spiny armor, provides protection that also keeps love and nurturing at bay. Notice whether the shields that other people wear are really effective. . . . Now consider your own shields (how you feel inside your own protective armor), and determine whether or not they are really working for you at this time in your life. . . . [*Pause.*]

Turn around, and you will find yourself standing on the hot sands of a high desert, a dry, rocky place dotted with brush, scrubby trees, and cacti. There is a horned lizard looking up at you from a rock. As you observe the features of this lizard and see how he is protected by his points and horns, you realize just how impressive your own defenses are, especially now that they are physically manifest. . . .

Horned Lizard tells you the tale of his evolution. He didn't create his horns as protection against the dangers of childhood; they're part of his ongoing evolutionary process. . . . [*Pause.*]

Share your story with the lizard now, the story of how you created your magnificent spines. . . . [*Long pause.*]

Now you have the opportunity to relinquish parts of your coat of armor if you so choose. You can give any shields that you are ready and willing to release to Horned Lizard, and he will find a way to incorporate them into his DNA. Take the time you need to do this and observe the transfer. . . . [*Pause.*]

Free of the shields that you have chosen to release, you notice that all of your sensitivities have become heightened. . . . Take some time to integrate this new vulnerability and get comfortable with it. Be aware that your new level of sensitivity will help you recognize the presence of real danger—a useful skill that will protect you without walling you off from others.

Thank the lizard for the wonderful lesson you have received, and turn around. You find yourself back in the crowd where you started, walking in your new skin and aware of your new vulnerability. You must use your new powers of discernment to thread a safe path through this crowd. . . .

Thoth is there and shares this new way of being with you.

[*When you are ready, Thoth will assist you back into your body. . . . Be sure to ground and center. . . .*]

WOLF
True Security

Many Native American traditions respect Wolf as a wise teacher and guide who has a remarkable sense of community. In Norse mythology he is legendary as Fenrir, the fierce wolf feared even by the gods, although in the wild Wolf is known to avoid confrontations. Wolf is a great teacher and companion who commands respect wherever he lives. He expresses the definitive canine qualities, including loyalty, friendship, and devotion to community. He is a very complex being, and his teachings are profound and varied.

In this journey, Wolf helps you see the truth of where you are at the moment and gives you guidance that is pertinent to where you are headed. You can trust that it is always safe to work with him. However, if you think that you are successfully hiding something from the world, Wolf will see right through your ruse. You can always count on him to give you an authentic reflection of your self.

All of Wolf's senses are extremely acute. When he places his head close to the ground, he can sense the vibrations of all that is happening in the earth below. His ears distinguish noises that don't even register in human awareness. With his acute sensitivity he hears you speak and can distinguish truth from falsehood, for there is a certain resonance that happens only when someone speaks his or her truth. When you speak only from your head, disconnected from your emotions and body wisdom, your message doesn't resonate with Wolf, but when you speak from your gut or your heart, he hangs on every word. You will be able to tell which you are doing because Wolf will become impatient, nervous, and tense if you speak only from your intellect. He relaxes when he hears the emotional language of the heart.

Wolf can also smell every odor that you emit. He is extremely perceptive and knows the exact state of your mind and heart at any given moment, so be attentive to your thoughts when you are visiting him—his penetrating eyes can see right into the center of your soul.

When you journey to visit Wolf, he will help you find your true source of strength and security. He invites you to walk away from refuge and safety to discover who you really are. Security comes when you give up your attachment to your safe haven, whether it is a physical place or old beliefs or habits. As soon as you relinquish the old form, then something new can happen. It is only through seeking the truth that we can initiate change. Your decision to take this journey is a message to the universe that you are no longer content with maintaining the illusion of security; you are ready to find the true source within.

One of the most important gifts of this journey is the invitation to see your own truth through the unflinching eyes of Wolf, who witnesses and accepts the reality of all he sees.

Wolf Journey

[*Do the alchemy. . . .*]
Thoth directs you to a campfire in a small clearing deep in the woods. It's nighttime, and you are all alone, sitting on a log. You are aware of the texture of the bark as you run your hand over the log's surface. Note the stability of your seat. . . . Feel the warmth of the fire and look up at the flickering light playing on the branches of the trees all around you. This space by the fire feels safe and warm. The flames burn brightly, and should they die down, there is plenty of wood stacked nearby. It is very quiet.

You feel a presence; as you look toward it you see two yellow eyes peering at you from the darkness, just outside the circle of light. Even though you have invited him, it is still important to notice how you feel when you see the eyes of Wolf. With a glance back into the darkness, he invites you to follow him.

Walk toward Wolf. As you get to the edge of the circle of light, he gives you a brief look, then turns to enter the dark forest. You must leave the campfire, and all it represents, in order to follow him as he moves slowly ahead. It's very quiet and extremely dark, for the understory of this huge forest has been shaded from the light for centuries. You find yourself adjusting easily to the darkness. . . . You may find your own physical movements becoming more like those of the wolf. Follow him into the forest. . . . Dim shapes of trees loom all around you as the campfire recedes. As you penetrate the woods, notice your senses sharpening—your ears are alert for any sound, your eyes probe for movement, and your nose samples the air for the smells around you as you come more into connection with the wolf spirit inside of you.

Just ahead of you the wolf walks slowly forward. After some time, he stops by a fallen log next to a large tree. Find yourself a place to sit on the log. The wolf sits on his haunches nearby. He is absorbed by all he perceives in the forest and invites you to experience this moment as he does. Allow your mind to follow any sensations, for Wolf has created an open, safe space to allow you to receive a teaching from the forest. . . . [Long pause.]

An owl swoops past, her velvet wings almost touching you as she flies silently by. You may be startled or even frightened until you realize she is on her own hunt.

Return your attention to Wolf, whose penetrating gaze is turned upon you. Allow yourself to know who you are at this moment, without any overlay of description or story, releasing your attachment to what you believe about yourself, for this is how Wolf perceives you. . . . [Pause.] Now you have an opportunity to ask Wolf any question that comes into your mind. Even if the wolf answers with silence, you know that the world will answer your question in some other way.

Wolf suddenly stands up, gives you a knowing glance that communicates the experience you have just shared, and bids you farewell until next you call upon him. He turns quickly and walks into the underbrush. You know you are not to follow. Alone in the dark, allow your senses to extend beyond what you can see and hear, and know that you can find the way back to your campfire. The spirit of the wolf within lets you access Wolf's acute consciousness and move through the forest with confidence. Sense the fire's warmth and follow it through the trees, through the darkness, until you begin to see its glow.

You are bringing what you have learned back to the campfire. Thoth is there, welcoming you. In the circle of warmth, you stir the embers.

Pick up the log that you sat on at the start of the journey and offer it into the fire. Discuss your experience with Thoth and ask him any questions that may have come up for you. . . .

[*Thoth will assist you back into your physical body. . . . Ground and center. . . .*]

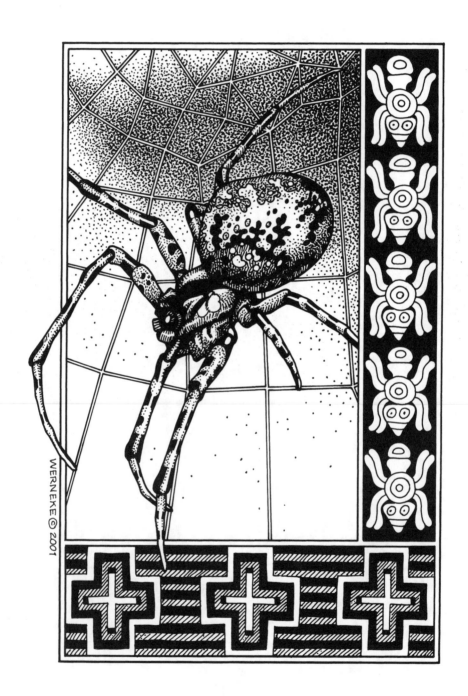

SPIDER

Awe/Weaving the Creation

Grandmother Spider has been revered by many indigenous cultures as the weaver of the universe. The Lakota Indians call her "Iktome," weaver of the healing power. Spider teaches us how to endure within our present reality while at the same time comprehending our individual relationship to creation in its entirety—her web is a metaphor for the thoughts that express our inner landscape. Many consider Grandmother Spider to be the oldest being; in some traditions our world came into existence as a result of the web she wove in the Beginning. In India, Spider is associated with *maya*, that is, the illusion of our three-dimensional reality.

We all spin webs of energy that we project into the world in all directions and through all dimensions. Like the silken threads spun from the substance of the spider's own body, each of our energy waves carries our unique vibration or signature. These patterns are the composite of everything we are and know and have touched. We sing this vibratory song of ourselves to everything, and everything sings back to us, defining our individual place in the cosmos.

Spiders communicate with one another by plucking on different strands of their webs, which sets up vibrations that are seen, felt, and heard throughout the universe. The slightest vibration registers across the web. All this information is shared—endlessly.

The center of the universe for each spider is wherever that spider stands on its individual web. Spider knows how to walk her own web— which threads to grasp and which to avoid. She doesn't step on the sticky threads where she could be easily trapped. You'll notice that

Spider does not place sticky threads at the center of her web, for that is the center of her self. Some of our thoughts are sticky also, and they can entangle us in the way that Spider's sticky threads ensnare her prey. Other thoughts, like the framework of her web, are strong and structural. By example, Spider teaches us about discernment—she helps us know which thoughts to hang on to and which to pass by. Spider is always watchful, as you must be when you travel with her.

The sticky threads of Spider's web can be compared to the material structure of the world—maya, the illusion. Spider uses those sticky threads to make her living, just as you must make your living by playing with the illusion. But as those who are experienced at meditation are aware, the only thing we truly know is the transient nature of our thoughts. Spider teaches you to relate to your mind as she relates to her web. You can always call on Spider for clarity of vision when you feel caught in the threads of your mind and the maya of our three-dimensional reality.

Lesser known but equally profound is Spider's gift as healer. Science tells us that, pound for pound, a spider's silk is stronger than steel. One teaspoon of this fine silk can weave one million webs! Indigenous wisdom tells us that fresh webs were used to cover wounds before we had Band-Aids. Using the same kind of silk she uses to wrap her prey, Spider can mend tears in both internal and external tissue and weave a web that can hold a tenuous healing in place during recovery. Once you have developed a relationship with Spider, you can call on her for healing assistance.

Spider has been weaving Creation since long before anything we recognize came into existence. . . . Our natural response to her alien nature runs the gamut from awe to terror to repulsion. When we journey with Spider, we have an unusual opportunity to just be with the sensation of awe. Because Earth is constantly moving through the universe, we enter the domains of different weavers as our planet's location changes. This means that every time you take the spider journey, you will meet a new spider and be shown something entirely different.

Spider Journey

[Do the Cauldron alchemy and come into the presence of Thoth. . . .]
When you meet Thoth, he is standing on one strand of a huge web, of which you can see only a small portion from your vantage point. As your attention focuses on the silken strand, you can hear the vibration of the web and see how that vibration sets up a pattern of light. You can imagine how this web vibration moves out into the universe and interacts with other webs. . . .

Take a moment to notice where you are in relation to these other webs. . . . *[Pause.]*

Reach out and touch the strand. Instantly you become part of the web and, zing, you shoot straight up the filament, right out of our atmosphere and into the center of this giant, cosmic web. . . .

When you rematerialize, you find yourself face to face with a giant spider. Notice that you perceive only a portion of the spider, for part of her is always in another dimension. As she spins her web, she creates the maya that we recognize as our three-dimensional reality. Pay attention to Spider as she spins out a new thread. From her weaving, space and time are created. Watching her weave, you realize you don't have to be trapped by our mere three-dimensional reality. With this recognition of infinite, simultaneous possibility comes the realization that everything is interconnected.

Now you have the opportunity to let go of your individual identity and receive the gift of Spider's perspective. From where she stands, you can look not only back at Earth, but also out upon the rest of our solar system, our galaxy, and the cosmos beyond. You are on one of many billions of webs, each burgeoning and billowing in a frenzy of growth that is continuous and infinite. . . . *[Long pause.]*

Although Spider's vantage point is very different from our own, and much larger, it lets us see the connections between her individual web and all the other webs in the cosmos. Spider plucks one strand and sets her web vibrating. . . . Notice how this vibrating web intersects with all the other webs spun by other spiders. At each intersection is the nexus point where matter ignites and comes into form. The intersecting points give strength to the creation. The relationships among the billions of spiders that are spinning, plucking, and moving on their webs creates the galaxies, the stars, and the planets that we know to be our universe. . . .

Take a few moments to acknowledge and bear witness to the entire spectrum of existence. . . . [*Long pause.*]

Now, from this expanded perspective, Spider gives you an opportunity to look back at Earth without judgment and see what we as a species have created. With this perspective you can see what needs to be done in your arena of influence. When you return to the material plane, perhaps you will be able to offer new contributions. . . . [*Pause.*]

When your experience feels complete, be sure to give acknowledgment and appreciation to Spider for the insights you have received. . . .

To return to ordinary reality, begin to focus on being back in your individual world, at the center of your own universe. . . . Spider starts plucking the strands all around you, surrounding you with vibrations of light and sound. As the light and sound begin to solidify, they slowly take on the form of your everyday physical surroundings. . . .

Share your experience with Thoth and receive whatever information or message he has for you at this time. . . .

[*Thoth will assist you back into your ordinary consciousness. . . . Be sure to ground and center before opening your eyes. . . .*]

Mustang

Spirit of Freedom

Horses have been revered throughout history by many cultures including, the ancient Chinese, many European traditions, and Native Americans. They exemplify the spirit of freedom. And nothing embodies this spirit as well as the few remaining wild mustangs, who maintain a fierce independence. Horses are considered safe vehicles for travel in both the physical and spiritual worlds. Shamans ride their mustangs through the upper world and the lower world with equal facility.

Mustang's gift is the ability to live fully in the moment. The mustang journey is about the ride itself, not about going anywhere in particular. With his adventurous spirit, Mustang invites you to surrender yourself fully to the experience of life. Whenever you feel confined, you can climb onto Mustang's back, become one with your horse, know the joy of the wind in your hair, and fly. Mustang teaches you to trust in the moment and also a reminds you to recognize your own magnificence. Although you can take this journey any time, I chose Mustang for the final journey in this new edition in order to culminate with the powerful, exhilarating experience of freedom.

Mustang Journey

[*Do the Cauldron alchemy and connect to Thoth. . . .*]
Thoth points to the sky, where you see beautiful, billowing white clouds. As you admire the shifting cloud patterns, the shape of a horse emerges. . . . You wonder what it would be like to jump onto the back of this great horse and ride. As soon as this thought forms in your mind, the cloud horse drops down to the ground and becomes a pinto stallion,

galloping at the head of a herd of wild mustangs. You find yourself in a vast meadow surrounded by rolling hills. The herd of mustangs thunders by, racing the wind with joyous abandon.

As the horse from the clouds leads the mustangs through the meadow, allow yourself to feel the desire to run free with the herd. You call out, "Help me to be free, help me to know freedom." The lead horse hears your call and stops—he turns to face you but keeps his distance. . . . Become very still. . . . Without moving, you and the horse observe each other. In order to ride this horse, you must gain his trust; he must gain yours in return. To give him time, remain perfectly still, with your heart open. Maintain this neutral space as the horse slowly, slowly inches his way toward you.

Finally this magnificent mustang stands directly in front of you. Stay quiet and focus on the horse. He circles your body once before coming around to face you. Then he nods in recognition—you have become present enough to receive his gift. With his permission, you mount, swinging easily onto his bare back. As you grab hold of his mane, he starts to move slowly, then breaks into a lope, heading out to catch up with the herd. . . . Lean over his neck and feel his body rippling under you. You are aware of his strength, his sure sense of direction, and his joy in the run. Allow yourself to merge with the horse, to fully experience this moment as he does. . . . [*Pause.*]

As soon as Mustang feels that you are one with him, he breaks into a gallop, bounding across the meadow and over the hills, then leaping into the air and flying up and up, into the clouds and beyond. Feel the wind sweeping by and experience this exquisite sense of freedom. Enjoy your ride. . . . [*Long pause.*]

When you feel complete with your journey, you fly back down through the atmosphere and through the clouds, until you and the mustang touch the earth. You return to the place where Mustang found you and dismount. Looking up, you see an eagle circling overhead. It drops a beautiful, spotted eagle feather, which you retrieve with gratitude and tie to the mane of your magnificent, magical mustang as your gift of appreciation. . . .

Thoth is there waiting for you. Take a moment to share your experience with him. . . .

[*Thoth will help you back into your physical body and ordinary consciousness. Be sure to ground and center. . . .*]

AFTERWORD

With completion comes gratitude,
and here we give thanks to
all our relations.

WERNEKE © 1991

The Garden
Gratitude/Looking Beyond

The garden is a place of fulfillment, which becomes the platform that leads to the next level, or stage, in your development. You can use the serenity of this garden to envelop yourself in the peace necessary to look beyond the limitations of your hopes and dreams. If you are still hoping for things, you won't be able to see the future. As long as your energy is concerned with things that you want, that you don't think you can have or achieve, you remain stuck. Once you experience getting all that you desire—experiencing it, loving it, receiving it joyously—then what? Let the unforeseen be the final gift from the Cauldron, and you can return from time to time to experience your own growth and changes and the as-yet inconceivable possibilities that await you.

This journey provides an opportunity to enrich your relationship with the totems you have encountered in this book. It provides a space for reconnecting with and honoring your newfound allies. In my own journey with these and other spirit friends, I have experienced spontaneous connections with these beings simply for the purpose of expressing thanks. The gratitude and joy felt during this process have evoked some of my deepest and most heartfelt moments.

You need not wait to come to this garden until you have met every participant in *Power Animal Meditations*, for this journey will nourish you any time.

Garden Journey

[*Do the Cauldron alchemy.* . . .]
Thoth is there. He is very happy to see you and brings you to a lush, full garden. Take a moment for a special honoring of Thoth so that you can thank him for his guidance through these journeys. . . . [*Pause.*]

Afterword

❦ ❦ ❦ ❦ ❦ ❦ ❦

As you enter the garden, you might see the Crone tending a rosebush as appropriate to the season. She is also delighted to see you. She may point out some of the special plants or new additions. The love that the Crone feels for you is like the love she feels for this garden. You may wish to share appreciation and love for one another. . . . [*Pause.*]

There are many flowers, shrubs, medicinal and culinary herbs, and fruit trees, yet this garden is constantly changing and growing, and within its unique design is a path of self-awareness. As you move between the beds and among its lush foliage, your senses heighten. Smell the fragrances, including those of the rich soil, the herbs, and the flowers. Listen to the sounds of the insects, bees, and humming-birds. . . .

A place for you to sit is provided in a spacious area in the center of the garden. Notice what is growing immediately around you. . . .

Allow time for each of the animals and other allies from your experiences within *Power Animal Meditations* to come into the center of the garden. This is a special time for honoring and gratitude. Most will pay their respects and leave after your sharing time. Some will stay for a while, usually to let you know they have further work to do with you. . . . [*Long pause.*]

When love and thanks are fully shared and farewells are complete, start to think about what you would like to have occur next in your life. Choose some aspect of your life that is very important to you, that you would like to develop. Be open to having a variety of possibilities unfold, and decide on that which is your heart's desire, your highest hope for the future. Focus on what it would be like to receive exactly what you want to have happen in your life, and to bring that into fruition. . . . Be there with it in the garden. Imagine that you have already received it. Accept that it has already transpired. . . . What does the world around you look like and feel like? . . .

Once you see yourself as having that which you desire, then something else can come into existence as a result. So accept that you have it, and then see what takes place next. Now you can have a taste of what it will be like in the future. Be ready for the unexpected. . . . [*Pause.*]

[*Take as long as you need. You know the way back. . . .*]

ABOUT THE AUTHOR

Nicki Scully's personal journey began in New York on June 19, 1943. She spent her formative years in southern California before opting for the adventure and excitement of the Bay Area in the late 1960s. It was during this time that she met Rock Scully, then manager of the Grateful Dead, with whom she lived until 1981. This relationship immersed her in the world of music and events within which energetic alchemy was a way of life. Out of that psychedelic cauldron, she emerged with a new understanding of the sacred and the motivation to explore her life's work in the fields of healing and metaphysics.

In 1969, Nicki was introduced to shamanic healing in the Native American tradition and has continued to study and honor Native American religious and traditional ways.

A deep interest in Egypt led Nicki to make several trips to that country in 1978 and 1979. Her explorations created a physical link to the ancient culture whose relevant truths are brought forward in her current work. She now leads tours to Egypt for serious students who want to experience initiations at the temples.

In 1981, Nicki moved to Eugene, Oregon, and was initiated to the first two degrees of Reiki by the late master Bethel Phaigh. Direct access to energy for healing served to redirect her life to the alleviation of pain and suffering. A study of Huna followed, and out of that work came her direct connection to her mentor and teacher, the Egyptian god of wisdom, Thoth, with whom she has been working ever since. Together they created this book, *Power Animal Meditations,* and the form that her healing work has taken, Alchemical Healing.

Nicki's unique work has found expression in her healing practice and seminars, her audiocassette tapes and CDs (see pages 264–65), and this book. She combines energetic healing techniques with shamanic principles to provide integrated and balanced healing and growth processes. She currently lectures and teaches seminars throughout the world and takes groups to Egypt and other sacred power places for direct experience of the sacred.

For more information about Nicki Scully and her tours and seminars, see www.shamanicjourneys.com.

ABOUT THE ARTIST

Angela Werneke's life journey continues to be an ever deepening exploration of the alchemy of word and image as it serves personal and planetary healing. This exploration has found expression through the vehicles of design, illustration, writing, and astrology, wherein Angela works with the idea that myth and metaphor serve as gateways to other dimensions. It is her perspective that, as we expand the territory we are willing and able to journey, we come to realize and cherish our interconnectedness with all life.

Angela's work as a designer and illustrator is represented in *Medicine Cards,* a divination system based on animal wisdom, as well as in a variety of other books and media that in some way further healing on the earth. The intent of her creative contribution to these works has been to bridge the other-than-human beings of the natural world to collective human awareness and awaken a respect and compassion for all life.

Applying the principles of alchemy, myth, and metaphor to astrological counseling, Angela works with planetary relationships in the horoscope as sacred geometry, using the image it suggests as a metaphor for the dynamics of the chart. In addition, she incorporates celestial mythology to illuminate story and life purpose. The intent of this approach is to support personal evolutionary process and more clearly define the soul's work.

Angela lives in northern New Mexico in the midst of a lively community of rocks, trees, plants, animals, and humans, where she nourishes a deepening relationship to place, purpose, and the next spiritual passage.

AUDIOCASSETTE TAPES AVAILABLE
FROM NICKI SCULLY

The following tapes function as audio illustrations for
Power Animal Meditations:

The Cauldron of Thoth, a Journey of Empowerment
With music by John Sergeant
Side one: Initiation—The Cauldron and the Crone
Side two: Music only
Nicki Scully, 1987

The Cauldron Teachings: Journey with Eagle & Elephant
With music by Roland Barker
Side one: Journey with Eagle & Elephant
Side two: Music only
Nicki Scully, 1989

The Cauldron Journey for Healing
With music by Roland Barker and Jerry Garcia
Side one: Journey for Healing with Kuan Yin
Side two: Music only
Sahalie Publishing, 1990

Proceeds from the sale of this tape will go toward the production and distribution of more of these tapes to be *given away* to people with AIDS, leukemia, or cancer or to centers and practitioners working with those diseases. Donations are tax deductible.

The Cauldron Journey for Rebirth
With music by Roland Barker and Jeff Mahoney
Side one: Journey for Rebirth with the Hippopotamus Goddess Tarät
Side two: Music only
Nicki Scully, 1991

Awakening the Cobra
With music by Roland Barker
Side One: Journey with the Cobra for Clearing the Chakras
and Awakening the Kundalini Energies.
Side Two: Music only
Nicki Scully, 1992

CDS AVAILABLE FROM NICKI SCULLY

Tribal Alchemy

Three journeys are available on this CD: Renewal, Journey for Peace,
and Animal Totems

Music produced and arranged by Roland Barker

Nicki Scully, 1996

. . . And You Will Fly!

An Animal Circus Adventure

Written by Nicki Scully, Roland Barker, and Mark Hallert

Narrated by Nicki Scully

Music written and produced by Roland Barker

Sahalie Publishing, 2001

An alchemical healing story produced as a radio play for children to be given away *free* to any child suffering from a potentially terminal disease and to those hospitals and practitioners working with these children. Proceeds from the sale of this CD will go toward further production and distribution so that more can be given away.

To order, contact your local bookseller or
Nicki Scully
P.O. Box 5025
Eugene, OR 97405
nscully@shamanicjourneys.com
www.shamanicjourneys.com

BOOKS OF RELATED INTEREST

SACRED GEOMETRY ORACLE DECK
by Francene Hart

MEDITATIONS WITH ANIMALS
A Native American Bestiary
by Gerald Hausman

WALKING ON THE WIND
Cherokee Teachings for Harmony and Balance
by Michael Garrett

THE WORLD IS AS YOU DREAM IT
Shamanic Teachings from the Amazon and Andes
by John Perkins

PSYCHONAVIGATION
Techniques for Travel Beyond Time
by John Perkins

ORIGINAL WISDOM
Stories of an Ancient Way of Knowing
by Robert Wolff

DANCE OF THE FOUR WINDS
Secrets of the Inca Medicine Wheel
by Alberto Villoldo and Erik Jendresen

CENTERING
A Guide to Inner Growth
by Sanders Laurie and Melvin Tucker

Inner Traditions • Bear & Company
P.O. Box 388
Rochester, VT 05767
1-800-246-8648
www.InnerTraditions.com

Or contact your local bookseller